# MY
# WHISPERING
# ANGELS

In October 1999, FRANCESCA BROWN was diagnosed with ME and was virtually bedridden for two years. However, in 2001 an Angel appeared to her and helped to heal her illness. She made a full recovery and Francesca has been in daily contact with the Angels ever since, and she continues to work with them as a conduit to those in need. She lives in Spain and is married with two children.

# MY WHISPERING ANGELS

## FRANCESCA BROWN

HODDER

First published in Great Britain in 2009 by Hodder & Stoughton
An Hachette UK company

First published in paperback in 2010

5

A CIP catalogue record for this title
is available from the British Library

ISBN 978 0 340 99495 5

Typeset in Plantin Light by Ellipsis Books Limited, Glasgow

Printed and bound in the UK by CPI Group (UK) Ltd, Croydon, CR0 4YY

Hodder & Stoughton policy is to use papers that are natural, renewable
and recyclable products and made from wood grown in sustainable forests.
The logging and manufacturing processes are expected to conform
to the environmental regulations of the country of origin.

Hodder & Stoughton Ltd
338 Euston Road
London NW1 3BH

www.hodder.co.uk

*To all the beings of light who take this journey.*
*May your Angels be always by your side.*

# Acknowledgements

I am forever thankful for the love and support from the Angelic realm which has opened up my life to a new way of thinking and living. Without it this book would never have been written.

I would also like to thank a wonderful light who was guided into my life so that this story could be told, my wonderful and dear friend Niall Bourke. To you I will always be grateful.

Also, I would like to thank Hachette Ireland, and the beautiful staff who work there, for believing in this story and for helping me to bring it to the world.

To the wonderful people I have met along the way, especially my sister Elaine who has been a wonderful mentor to me. She always encouraged me to keep going in times of doubt and she is a beautiful light in my life.

To the wonderful staff and officer of Irish Ferries' 'Oscar Wilde' who have brought sea travel to another level, and special thanks to my beautiful friend Paula.

To my two wonderful sons, Jason and Dwayne, for their love and understanding as the world of Angels came into their lives. Also thanks to their loving partners Maire and Dearbhla. And thanks to my wonderful husband Fran for all his love, support and encouragement in understanding that this journey with the Angels was important to me. Without him this journey would have been impossible.

Finally, I have to mention my wonderful and beautiful pet dogs who have travelled with me on this journey and have always been there for me. To Cassie Coco who still travels on. To Kissy and Holly who now live with the Angels.

Love and light,
Francesca Brown

# Contents

# Foreword

In the autumn of 2001 I was working as a journalist in Dublin and very much looking forward to a two-month trip to Australia that I had been planning for some time. During the week before my departure, I received a phone call at my newspaper office from a man who asked me if I would be interested in doing a story on a psychic housewife from west Dublin who communicates with angels.

To be honest, the last thing in the world I wanted to do was traipse up to some housewife's front door and ask her about her experiences with angels, as the only thing on my mind was finalising details for my impending trip. I received the phone call on a Thursday afternoon and was due to depart for Australia the following Tuesday. But my news editor got to hear about the phone call and told me to go along and speak with the woman in the hope that we might get some kind of humorous human-interest piece on her.

So, the next day I found myself outside a semi-detached house in a suburban estate in Blanchardstown in west Dublin. I knocked on the door and a rather large man with a shaven head opened it. He welcomed me and took me inside the house.

'This is my wife, Francesca,' he said, indicating a woman somewhere in her early forties I would guess.

She held out her hand and I shook it, but I was aware that she wasn't making eye contact with me. Instead she was gazing intently at the top of my head, with a quizzical look on her face.

'Why do I see kangaroos jumping around your head?' she asked. 'And there's the Sydney Opera House in the background. Have you just been to Australia or are you about to go.'

I was stunned; very few people knew about my trip and I didn't see any possible way that this woman, whom I had never set eyes on before, could have had any knowledge of it. My amazement must have shown clearly on my face because her husband shrugged, let out a laugh and said, 'See, I told you she was psychic.'

I really didn't know what to make of what had just happened but I stayed with Francesca for the best part of two hours, during which time she told me things about a close relative of mine who had recently passed on in tragic circumstances and about incidents that had happened in my personal life, information that she couldn't possibly have gleaned from any source I could think of.

Following that dramatic meeting I got to know Francesca and her husband Francis very well and I wrote several articles for Sunday newspapers about her psychic abilities and relationship with angels. I have stayed in touch with Francesca over the years and spent several periods with her and Francis in their home in Spain. During that time I have witnessed her relationship with the angels become clearer and stronger as she delivers their message for anyone interested in hearing it.

I became so intrigued and fascinated with Francesca's

life that I suggested she write this book, a project on which we have collaborated.

Having worked with Francesca, I would like to say she is one of the most ordinary, down-to-earth and likeable people it has been my pleasure to meet.

Niall Bourke
Dublin, June 2009

# Introduction

My name is Francesca Brown. I'm a 50-year-old house-wife, married with two children. I suppose many people would describe me as an 'angel therapist' or practitioner.

In truth, these titles don't mean a lot to me but I do communicate with angels every day and I do consider them to be my best friends. Indeed, the most important day of my life was when a beautiful angel called Anne appeared to me in my bedroom in January 2000 and informed me that she was going to heal me of a debili-tating illness that I had suffered with for almost two years. Just how she proceeded to do that is contained within the pages of this book.

Prior to this I really had no knowledge of angels. I'd read and heard of people who had a connection to angels since their childhood and angels appear to have been with them since they were very young indeed. If we look at the history of mankind we see that angels came to Joan of Arc, to Daniel in the lions' den, to Samson and to Mary the Mother of God. I'm not comparing myself to any of these but when I look at it now I have to say that, yes, they came to me too.

I'd heard of angels, of course, but I'd never really paid them that much attention. I suppose I thought that they were just a lovely notion – something you found in religious literature or the Bible. Prior to my experience with Angel Anne I would have considered anyone who thought they could communicate with angels to be, quite frankly, insane. I was an ordinary housewife from Dublin struggling to do the best I could for my family. I never had any interest in the spirit world, nor was I particularly religious. As a matter of fact I knew a few friends who were interested in things like tarot cards, fortune tellers and mediums but I could never really muster any great enthusiasm for any of it.

However, since the year 2000, when Angel Anne first introduced herself to me, my life has changed totally and utterly. I have spent practically every day in communication with angels. They have delivered a variety of messages to me in a number of different forms that aim to help people with fundamental problems confronting them regarding human existence. Problems concerning how we as ordinary people can access and gain greater knowledge of those areas that we all yearn to understand – love, beauty, truth and the existence of God.

One of the angels' central messages is that God loves all of us equally. More importantly, that God's love is available equally to all of us, in fact it is already contained within us all – we are literally one with God; there is no separation between us and our Creator, there never could be and there never has been. The angels help us to unlock the belief that we are in some way separate from God.

It is my hope that this book will help people to come closer to a simple truth that I have come to know and understand:

that God already exists within us. They can do this by listening to what the angels have to say directly to humanity. The angels realise that an illusion exists whereby human beings feel alone and separate from the source of what they really are – God. They also realise that this illusion is extremely real and very strongly held in place by our human minds. The good news is that the angels also know how to dismantle that illusion and this, in part, is what this book is about.

To this day I still have no real understanding of why the angels picked me to communicate with, but I do know this – if I can communicate with the angels, then so can anyone if they really want to. It's very hard to describe in words what having an angel or angels in your life is like. You may encounter many fantastic or even miraculous happenings. Or you may not. My own experience of angels is that they are wondrous beings of light and at the same time they are always a very subtle and gentle thing to behold.

Angels are a conduit between heaven and earth; they are messengers – God's messengers. They can help you with guidance, with wisdom, with your health and with your relationships with other people. Whatever your potential, wherever your journey takes you, you need only honestly open your heart to the angels and a new way of living and learning will result.

I've come to learn that angels cannot live your life for you but they are always present guiding and directing you; whether you realise it or not makes no difference. I believe angels are part of a timeless knowledge stored very deep inside each and every one of us; there they stand, just waiting to be awakened by you and to help you to remember that which you have forgotten but which is still there in your subconscious mind.

To make a connection with your angel is to return to that wondrous state that we all enjoyed when we were very young. It's a state of innocence and of purity but we've managed to cover over it with all the concerns of adulthood and modern living. I believe that somewhere deep within our subconscious minds we still retain that sheer sense of joy that we encountered as very young children as we stared out at our parents from our cot and gurgled with happiness for no particular reason.

In fact, I believe that even now, as people are reading these words, there is something in the back of their minds that still recognises the state I am talking about, that state of oneness with the source of everything. And what a wonder it is when we re-find that loving state within ourselves. I know that joyous state *can* be regained. One of the angels' main functions is to help human beings to return to their natural state; it is a state of pure being; a state of complete joy; a state of oneness with God.

This book is not intended to be a sort of angel manual – it's not an easy three-step guide to contacting your angels, although hopefully it will genuinely help people to make that initial contact with their own angel if that is what they desire. Rather, this book is my own story, the story of a woman from Dublin who, when she was very ill, suddenly and for no apparent reason made a wondrous connection with the angels. Making that connection has resulted in an amazing journey, not only for me but for my husband Fran and my two sons, Jason and Dwayne. Time has not and cannot diminish that connection; in fact, it has grown stronger and stronger as time has moved on.

This book is a record of the last nine years, since I started my journey with the angels. It's been a truly incredible time and I hope you enjoy the story.

# I

# A Glimpse of Heaven

I was born in the Rotunda Hospital in Dublin on 19 October 1958. My parents, John and Alice Gibbs, originally lived in the north Dublin suburb of Cabra before the family moved to nearby Finglas.

We were a normal working-class family I suppose. My father worked as a bus driver for Dublin Bus and my mother also worked part-time at different jobs. I had four brothers and sisters: Michael, Mark, Elaine and Jackie. I would say I had a relatively happy childhood. We never had a lot of money, but that wasn't very remarkable in itself, as nobody seemed to have a lot in those days.

I still have happy memories of long summer days spent at the seaside town of Rush on the north Dublin coast line, about 12 miles from our home. My dad had an old Morris Minor car and he would fill it up with as many of us as he could fit in and drive us all out to Rush. Then he would turn the car around and go back to Finglas and collect our neighbours, the Fitzpatricks, and their children and drive all the way back to Rush again. That was very typical of the times – neighbours seemed to be far friendlier and closer to each other than perhaps they are today.

We lived near the River Tolka in Dublin and that was a constant source of fun and adventure for all the kids of the neighbourhood. I remember swimming in the river during the summer so it must have been a lot cleaner than it is today. There were also a great many fields around Finglas when I was growing up; they are all gone now – replaced with housing estates. We'd often play till ten o'clock in the evening before my mother would call us back to our house.

Childhood gangs were important back then; everyone was in some kind of a gang, whether it was myself and a few girlfriends or my brothers who had their own gangs, and of course us girls were never allowed into any of the boys' gangs.

I can still recall the name of our local sweet shop on Cardiffsbridge Road in Finglas. It was called Morris's, owned by a man named Marty Morris. Every Friday evening, when my dad would come home from work, he'd give us a shilling and we would descend on Mr Morris's shop to buy sweets and crisps. An even bigger treat was on the occasional Friday when my elder brother Michael would be given the money to go to our local chip shop and buy fish and chips. If I stop and let my mind wander back I can still recall how good a smoked cod and chips tasted to us kids all that time ago – although we never got to eat a whole one.

Another thing that caused my siblings and I untold excitement was a trip to the local cinema. There was a cinema in Finglas when I was young and on Saturday after-noons between three and six they showed two films and maybe some cartoons. We'd walk down to the cinema; my brother Michael would be in charge and I can still remember the sheer joy and excitement of watching a western or a war film on the big screen. It was as if you were actually there in the trenches when a German soldier got shot or an American cavalryman got an Indian's arrow through his chest. I believe one of the first films I saw in the cinema was called *The Russians are Coming*.

It's remarkable the impressions that stay with you from your childhood, especially the happy memories. I still vividly recall being taken by my parents at Christmas time to the pantomime in St Francis Xavier Hall on Dublin's Quays. The Widow Twanky and the Ugly Sisters seem as real in my mind's eye today as they did when we screamed at the top of our lungs, 'He's behind you!' all those years ago.

Looking back on it now, I can always remember a certain presence in my life. I don't know how best to describe it: it was a subtle feeling yet a very definite feeling. I knew I was being watched over. I'd often sense it when I was alone; it just felt as if there was someone else there, although I couldn't see anyone. At different times in my young life – perhaps I was having a hard time at school, or maybe there wasn't a lot of money around and my parents were worried about providing for the family – I'd have this sense that things were going to be alright. In fact it was more than a sense – I knew things were going to be alright. I would gather my brothers and sisters around me and tell them not to worry: we were being looked after.

I always loved the outdoors and I can remember having this great affinity with the sky and the starry heavens from a very young age. I just adored staring up into the vast universe and gazing in wonder at the sheer size and majesty of it all. I loved to gaze up and let it overwhelm me to the point that I felt I was insignificant and somehow had become a part of the stars as they twinkled and shone their amazingly gentle light down on me. I don't know if people thought I was odd; perhaps they did.

I can still recall looking up at the sky one lovely summer's evening. I was out in one of the fields close to our house and it had just got dark and the stars had begun to peep out. As I gazed up at the heavens I had this strange sense that up there was where I really came from, where I really belonged. I felt as if I had been dropped down here on earth and I had left someone or something that I really loved behind me up there in the sky. I remember feeling that I had something to do down here on earth and when I was finished I would return to the stars, return to my real home. As I gazed up I said out loud, 'If you're still up there then come and get me when I'm finished and ready to go home; please don't forget about me.' I can still remember that summer's evening as if it was yesterday.

I recall this strong sense of being looked over all through all my childhood. Often, when lying in bed before I dropped off to sleep, I'd feel a sense that there were many friends around me, really strong, good friends, although my sisters were the only ones with me in my bedroom.

One evening I had an encounter that I will never forget. Now I know you have to be very cautious about the memories and experiences of a very young child, but this incident made such an impression on me that it lodged in my mind and has stayed firmly with me to this day. I had just drifted off to sleep but something made me wake up again. As I looked straight ahead I could see three figures standing in front of my bed. They stood there, looking down on me. There were two older people, a woman and a man, and also a younger man. They were dressed in what looked to me like rather old clothes. But it was their presence that totally captivated me. The moment I saw them I wasn't in the slightest bit afraid; there was a sense of great peace about them, a very gentle, warm feeling of peace and security. I felt the urge to jump out of bed and greet them, to hug them, the same as you would if your favourite auntie had just walked into the room and you were delighted to see her.

The three figures just stood there looking at me. I could feel they really cared about me – they really loved me. I eventually asked them who they were. The woman answered, 'I am Mary. This is my husband Joseph and this is our son Jesus. Don't be afraid, we are here to look after you.' What was strange was the sensation I had as she was talking. I realised that I knew the people were exactly who the woman said they were, even before she finished speaking. She didn't say anything else and I don't remember whether they took their leave of me or I fell asleep. What I do remember is waking the next morning, jumping out of bed and frantically looking around my room to see if they were anywhere to be found. I even looked under the bed. My sisters must have thought I had gone completely mad. I never forgot that night or the feeling of peace, love and security that I experienced while my three visitors were present.

I feel that what happened to me that night was my first conscious experience of the love of God. I wasn't left afterwards with any great devotion or even a great interest in Jesus, Mary and Joseph. I would often see images of them in religious books or when in church at Mass with my parents, but they meant nothing to me. I would also hear their names being mentioned by my school teachers and a local parish priest would come and talk to us each month on religious matters and often mention them, but none of that had any real effect on me. I didn't identify with any of it. What did affect me was the way I felt while in their presence; that is what stayed with me. I feel that same love and security now as I write these words; it doesn't go away.

Looking back now, I would say that experience sustained me for many years to come. No matter how hard things got I was always able to fall back on it although I never met those three wondrous figures again. I wasn't ever able to tell anyone what I had seen or experienced on that night in my bedroom, I just instinctively knew not to mention it to anyone. I knew they wouldn't understand. I felt in a way that I had been given that experience to strengthen me and to help my brothers and sisters.

I left school when I was sixteen and went to work in a big factory that manufactured cigarettes on the south side of Dublin city. I liked the work and made many friends in the factory from big Dublin working-class areas like Ballyfermot, Crumlin and Inchicore. At the weekends we'd do the usual things teenage girls did – go dancing and hope to meet some nice boys. Later on, I began to take the occasional drink and a big group of us would all meet up in certain pubs before we'd head on out to a disco in the city centre. They were happy times and I am still friends today with some of the girls I used to work with back then.

I met my husband Fran when I was twenty-one. It was on a Halloween night, 31 October 1979, and a group of us had decided we would all go to a fancy dress party being held in a hotel in Howth on the north side of Dublin. Fran was there, dressed in a massive gorilla suit and I was dressed as a footballer. Things didn't really get off to a great start between the pair of us because a few of my friends happened to be smoking at the table next to where Fran and his friends where sitting. One of Fran's friends turned and asked the girls if they would mind putting out their cigarettes as it was annoying him. Now this was a very long time before smoking in social settings was frowned upon, so he was quickly told that if he didn't like it he could always move to another table. So, to show solidarity with their friend, Fran and all the other young men at the table got up and moved away. This didn't bother us girls one bit; rather, we saw it as a small victory for women's rights – all a bit juvenile, but then we were all very young.

It wasn't long before Fran came back over to our table and asked me up to dance. I was delighted, although I didn't let him know it. I really liked Fran from the moment I first spoke to him; he made me laugh, he was gentle and kind and I remember saying to myself that night, 'This guy has a good heart and I can trust him.'

Physically, he was an impressive sight: broad shoulders and very well built, about six feet in height with blond hair. I remember thinking to myself that he must play a lot of football because he looked so fit. We hit it off straight away and decided we would meet up the next weekend. There's a traditional place for young couples to meet in the centre of Dublin known as Clery's Clock – Clery's being a well-known department store in the city centre.

At 8pm there I was, standing under Clery's Clock. I stood and I stood, but there was no sign of Fran. After what seemed like an eternity, but was perhaps fifteen minutes, I decided to call it a day and put the whole thing down to experience – a bad experience. I returned home muttering not very nice things about Fran and about men in general. After I'd been home perhaps an hour, our next-door neighbour knocked on our door to say there was a phone call for me. We didn't have a phone in those days and we would often use our neighbours' phone. I'd forgotten that I'd given Fran the number. He apologised profusely and explained that he was serving with the Irish Army and had been called away on an army exercise that he couldn't get out of.

When I decided that he had suffered enough I agreed to make another date for the following weekend. Almost immediately I tumbled head over heels in love with Fran and what followed was a six-week whirlwind romance, during which we had a wonderful time together going to the cinema and theatre or just out walking together. I felt ecstatically happy when I was with Fran and even though we had only known each other a matter of weeks we both knew we were meant for each other and we quickly became engaged.

I remember my mother's first question was 'Are you pregnant?' when I told her I was going to marry Fran. I assured her that wasn't the case but Fran and I knew we would both have a long hard road ahead of us and we'd have to save very hard before we could actually afford to get married.

Once I got to know Fran I realised that I was wrong about him playing a lot of football; it wasn't football that had him looking so fit, it was amateur boxing. I also learned something straight away – I had better get to like watching the sport of boxing because Fran was a very good boxer and he fought practically every week.

He boxed for the Transport Boxing Club in Dublin's north inner city and also for the Irish Army, and he took his training very seriously. Most Friday nights he had a boxing match in a sports arena called the National Stadium on the south side of Dublin. I remember the sheer fright I got when I first saw him have a really rough fight; he was covered in blood and his eye was swollen. What was really remarkable was just how quickly he could recover from a fight: the next day he would be looking almost normal again. He often explained to me that if you were really fit you could recover from almost anything.

We had to save very hard in order to get married and secure a deposit for a house. One of the ways we made it happen was by Fran opting to serve with the Irish Army in the Lebanon for six months. Off he went and I remember it being a very lonely time and missing him dreadfully. In terms of making money it worked and when he returned we did get married, in September 1981. I was twenty-three and soon after our wedding we moved into our first home in Deanstown Road, Finglas – across the road from where my mother and father lived.

I'd always wanted to have a little boy to love and look after, so you can imagine my delight and joy when Fran and I were blessed with two sons, Jason and Dwayne. I had Jason when I was twenty-five, after two years of marriage, and Dwayne followed two years later. When I say that our two little boys were full of energy I'm not joking; there never seemed to be enough hours in the day for them to run around the house or to kick a football. They could, and regularly did, wear me out, but I loved every minute of it.

It was a particularly happy period in my life. Things seemed to be working out just as I had imagined and hoped that they would: I had found myself a man I truly loved, married him and now I had two wonderful little boys to care for.

We also had a large group of friends, many of whom we had known since we were in our teens and we would meet regularly, mostly on Wednesday and Sunday nights, in a small pub we all loved in Cabra, north Dublin. The children coming along didn't seem to interfere with our social life at all; most of our friends also had young kids and in those days we always seemed to be able to arrange for babysitters. It was easier back then to get someone you could trust to look after the kids, and you wouldn't have to pay them the earth to do it.

You can imagine our horror when, at the age of two, Jason developed a serious medical condition known as Perthes disease (Legg-Calvé-Perthes syndrome). The disease attacks the ball part of the ball-and-socket hip joint, which gradually weakens and dies from a lack of blood supply. It was my mother who first noticed that he was dragging his leg a little and appeared to be in some discomfort. At first we thought that it might be the new pair of shoes that we had just bought him but we soon realised that it was not. We took Jason to Temple Street Children's

Hospital in central Dublin where they took X-rays and put his leg into traction for two weeks to see if that would correct the problem. When it didn't they decided they would have to operate and insert pins into his hip. It was a particularly difficult time for me as I had just given birth to Dwayne, whom I had to leave in the care of my mother as Fran and I looked after Jason.

After his operation they had to sedate Jason to keep him quiet and his leg and hip were in traction for over six weeks. When he did eventually come home he was in a wheelchair and later on he had to wear a brace in order to keep his bad leg up from the ground. We joked that he looked a little like 'Long John Silver'. A worry that we had at the time was that the doctors told us that there was a possibility that the condition might spread to Jason's other leg. There was also a possibility that he might be left with a permanent limp so we were monitoring him very closely and we were very worried.

The whole series of events surrounding the birth of Dwayne and Jason getting ill had begun to really take its toll on me. I remember our district nurse calling in to see me one day and telling me I looked so exhausted that I should have a home-help for two days a week until I got back on my feet again. I accepted this offer gratefully and the lady turned out to be really adorable and a great help to me at that difficult time.

Our neighbours and friends from around Finglas very kindly put together a collection to send Jason to Lourdes. Fran went with Jason on the trip to keep costs down and I stayed at home with Dwayne. Jason and Fran had a wonderful time in Lourdes. I remember thinking at the time that the whole operation and recovery period had seemed to break Jason's spirit somewhat and he didn't seem to be the same child he was before the operation. But the trip away had done him the world of good. I had never forgotten the experience that I had had in my bedroom all those years before and I prayed to Our Lady to remember her promise to me that she would look after me. I asked her, if possible, to intercede on behalf of Jason so that he might make a full recovery. I was praying very hard while they were both in Lourdes and my prayers were answered. Jason did in time recover completely, although it was a very long process and we were back and forth with him to Temple Street Hospital for check-ups until he was fourteen years old.

The evening that Jesus, Mary and Joseph appeared to me in my bedroom had left an indelible impression with me and there were many times when I wished I was able to share it with other people, but I felt I couldn't. I sensed that people just wouldn't understand me. Looking back with hindsight, that experience had left me with a sense of compassion for other people that has stayed with me right through my life. When I say compassion I'm not sure it's the right word – for example, if I was watching television and something came on the news about some horrible crime or atrocity someone had committed I always felt I could see both sides of the situation. When others would see it as being very black or white, I would encounter that same sense of love and security I had felt on the night when I experienced the visitation, and I would somehow know that this was the right way to look at the situation – that this sense of love I felt was what is behind all people, whether they are considered to be good or bad by others. But I couldn't really share the experience with anyone, and when I did try and express this sense of compassion that was running through me I would receive funny looks or someone would make a comment, so I just kept quiet.

However, it wasn't the only spiritual experience that happened to me that I couldn't explain and felt it best to keep to myself. It was September 1993, and my father had become ill with cancer and had been very sick for the past year. I was standing in the kitchen of my house in Deanstown Road when I got the very strong impression that there was someone behind me, so I looked around but there was nobody there. However, the kitchen door was open and I could see out into our front room. I knew there was someone or something in the front room; I can't explain it, I just had this very strong sense of something being present in the room. Although I was apprehensive I began to walk towards the door; it was as if I was being drawn to it. As I got to the door I could see a light emanating from around the corner, so I walked into the room and looked to my left. What I saw was a truly amazing sight.

There was what I would describe as a shaft or column of light, perhaps six feet high, in the corner of the room. It was a brilliant white light and it glowed and shimmered but didn't move from the corner. Strangely enough I didn't feel frightened now. Then suddenly three words flashed into my mind – 'Angel of Death'. Now I felt frightened. For some reason I didn't think of my father but rather of my own family, and I said, 'I hope you're not here for my husband or any of my children.' Then I heard a voice in my head say, 'I'm here for your father; his time to pass to the light is approaching fast but do not be afraid.' Then the light just faded away. I knew my dad was very ill and he wasn't expected to survive for very long but it was still shocking news. I felt tears begin to well up in my eyes and again I was left with the strong feeling I couldn't confide in anybody about what I had seen or been told.

My dad died on 21 October 1993. As the family, relations and friends gathered in my parents' house I had a strong urge to go across the road to my own home to be alone. As I entered my front room I knew the same presence that I had encountered five weeks previously was again present in the room. Sure enough, as I came into the front room and looked to the same corner of the room, there was the same light that I had encountered previously. It was brilliant and stunning as when I first saw it and as I looked at it I seemed to lose all fear again, and then I heard the same voice in my head, 'Don't be afraid, your father is now with his loved ones, he is happy and being looked after.' As the voice was speaking I had a wonderful feeling of release and of deep peace. I felt so grateful to know that my dad was with his loved ones and was being cared for. But then I sensed that the light was about to depart. 'Please don't go,' I blurted out. 'Please stay with me here for a while. I need you.' There was a still silence and then the voice spoke again. 'I have to go, my job here is done.' 'But will I ever see you again?' I asked. 'Please don't leave me by myself.' 'You won't see me again for a long time but you will see many more like me before too long,' came the reply and then the light just vanished. I was left alone in my house. A great many emotions were running through me. I felt alone and bewildered, but there was also a sense of relief of knowing that my dad was safe in the arms of the Lord and I gave thanks for that.

# 2

## The Healing Stones

In the mid-1990s, as our boys were beginning to get a little older, there was a lot of drugs and joy-riding going on in the Finglas area and the place was beginning to get a very bad name. What was really annoying about the situation was that the ordinary decent people of the area could do nothing to stop it. They felt helpless as they watched more and more problems develop in their neighbourhood, problems not necessarily being caused by the people who lived there.

Looking at what was going on and feeling as helpless as everyone else Fran and I decided we would move from Finglas if we could manage it. It was more for the boys' sake than for us. We did eventually manage to sell our home in Deanstown Road and on 31 April 1997 we moved to Blanchardstown, an area about three miles from Finglas. The move wasn't easy either financially or emotionally as we were leaving our friends and our lovely neighbours behind. But move we did, and we were really delighted with our new home and our new estate, where we quickly made new friends and had some lovely new neighbours.

I can't say I really remember the day that I started to feel ill. It was in the early days of January 2000. It was more a loss of energy and a feeling of listlessness that crept up on me. I had absolutely no idea that my world and that of family was about to be turned upside down for the next eighteen months. When I first noticed that I wasn't feeling right, and that simple things like going for walk or doing some dusting or hoovering began to feel like a great effort, I decided I would consult my local GP. I made my way down to the doctor's surgery and explained to him how I was feeling. He was very understanding and carried out a routine examination on me. He said he thought it was a muscular problem I was suffering with so he prescribed some anti-inflammatory drugs and told me to take it easy.

Another couple of weeks passed and I wasn't feeling any better, so I returned to the doctor. He examined me again and this time I could see he was more concerned. He told me he wanted me to attend Blanchardstown Hospital for some tests. The hospital wasn't far away from where we lived and I was beginning to feel so low that I readily agreed to attend in the hope that the tests would reveal something simple and I could get on with my life. But that's not what happened at all.

One set of tests came back and proved inconclusive, only to be followed by another set that revealed the same thing. I was back and forth between the hospital and my doctor like a yo-yo and all the time my energy seemed to be getting lower and lower. I had gone from being a fit, healthy mother of two, in her early forties and with a passion for walking and the outdoors, to being a bedridden, cranky sort of person who found getting up and preparing a meal for my husband and children beyond her capabilities.

The change that occurred in me over a period of perhaps

six months was quite remarkable. Previously, I had liked to go power-walking at a brisk pace for two or three miles at a time. I also loved to play squash, and a close friend and I would play pitch and putt once a week at a local course. All these activities came to a shuddering halt with the advance of my illness. I always considered myself to be an outgoing if not an over-confident person. I adored my family and had a very happy family life. I was always delighted to go and watch our sons playing football for their school or local club. As soon as we returned from one family holiday away I'd be looking forward to the next one. So I just couldn't grasp what was beginning to happen to me. I was left feeling more and more like an elderly person as the days went on.

At one stage my doctor broke the frightening news to me that he thought I might be developing the early stages of Multiple Sclerosis. Fran and I were really worried and the kids, who were in their early teens at the time, knew we were very worried about the situation, although they never said much about it.

After a number of tests, thankfully, my doctor told me I didn't have Multiple Sclerosis, but he thought I was suffering from ME. However, I have to say I felt that nobody really knew exactly what was wrong with me at the time. All I knew was that I was practically bedridden most days and I sometimes needed help even to go to the bathroom. Looking back on the illness now there are two things that remain foremost in my mind: the lethargy – that feeling of being like a lead weight and everything being a struggle; and also the aching muscles, especially in my legs. It's hard to explain the sheer sense of frustration of not being able to do the simplest things that everyone takes for granted.

I can't say that I actually became *severely* depressed but it was a constant battle to see the positive side of things. But I was determined to try and be positive, if only for the boys' sake. Fran was a rock throughout, although I knew it was taking a lot out of him as well. He was working as a taxi driver at the time and when he came in from working a long shift he then had to do all the housework and look after getting food on the table, as most of it was totally beyond me at the time.

I remember the afternoon that I first started to see the faces. I had spent the day, like so many before, just lying in bed bored. Fran and the boys had gone from the house and I was alone. We had a television in the bedroom and it had become something of a daily routine to watch the morning talk shows one after the other. I had begun to feel very cynical about some of the TV show hosts and I would find myself criticising them to myself. This was very unlike me, as before I would have looked forward to seeing some of these shows, even rushing home to make sure I didn't miss my favourite ones. Now they all seemed to have this same grey lustre to them; they seemed stupid and without any real purpose. But I still watched them – there wasn't anything else to do.

It was now early afternoon and I was lying in bed just staring out ahead of me, feeling miserable and contemplating if I would put the television back on for the afternoon shows, when I started to notice shapes forming in front of my vision. At first I didn't pay them all that much attention; I was feeling tired and drowsy at the time. But the shapes didn't go away, in fact they became more defined and took on the definite characteristics of people, just walking past me, ignoring me. When I realised just how realistic they were becoming, I started to become frightened of them.

At first, a lot of them seemed to come from – and I'm guessing here – maybe the 1800s; some looked like Victorian gentlemen with bowler hats and the women had long skirts and some of them had bonnets on their heads.

It was such a strange experience; the figures I was seeing in front of me were scary and I was now terrified by them, yet they were also fascinating, there was something compelling about them. It was as if I was being allowed a glimpse into this other world, which felt both real and unreal at the same time. The characters were all so clear, so defined in every detail, yet my rational mind was telling me that this couldn't be happening to me – I must be imagining it, or perhaps I was hallucinating. This went on for a couple of days and I didn't mention it to anyone. On one level I was intrigued at seeing these strange entities in front of me, but it was an intrigue very much tinged with fear, and I still had no idea where they were coming from. I didn't know whether I was imagining the whole thing or not. But, strangely, it was a slight relief just to have something happening in my life again after lying in bed for so long with nothing to do but watch television. All this changed on the third day of me witnessing the characters.

As I lay in bed and watched the various people come and go, something happened that totally shocked me. One of the characters – a man in a great black coat and a bowler hat – stopped, looked straight at me and addressed himself to me!

'You're not going to lay there for the rest of your life, are you?' he asked. I was terrified. While all these men and women had been walking by me minding their own business I felt relatively safe, although scared. But now this man had spoken to me. Was I losing my mind? I didn't know. I had the awareness that I was very sick and tired but at the same time I was aware that these characters appearing to me were very real. This made me feel slightly better. I seemed to be aware of my reality but there was this other dimension, these very real entities that were talking to me. I looked straight back at the man. I was frozen with fear. He looked at me, frowned and made a slightly irritated gesture, as if he was annoyed with me, and walked away.

The next day it happened again. Another man, this time with a grey beard and wearing what looked like peasant working clothes, stopped and said, 'Is it really that bad?' Then he smiled and walked on past. I was frightened and I had to say something to someone.

When I look back on the whole experience now I know that the characters I was witnessing in my bedroom were in fact my first glimpse into a psychic realm that exists in everyone's subconscious mind. As the years have gone by I've come to know and understand this realm intimately and I've also learned how to work with it in a positive way. Within this realm is contained many different phenomena and many ordinary people have glimpses of it but don't understand what is happening to them. For example, it is very common for people who have just lost a loved one to actually feel the presence of that person around them for quite some time after the person has died, and that intense feeling or presence comes from the realm I'm talking about. Indeed, it's a far more common occurrence than is generally acknowledged for people to see an actual image of someone who has just died, especially if they really loved the relative or friend. Of course, most people would refer to such an image as a ghost or spirit, but the image comes from the same psychic realm as the characters I was witnessing in my bedroom, although I didn't know it at the time. When people witness an image of a person close to them who has died it can be very frightening and so it was for me in those dark days of my illness when these unknown characters began to make themselves visible to me in my bedroom.

I knew Fran didn't know what to make of my story when I tried to explain what was happening. I think he was pretty sure I was hallucinating and this added greatly to his worry. He would often come home from work and exclaim, 'What in the name of God is going on, the place is lit up like a Christmas tree?' I would have every light on in the house because I was so scared of what was happening around me and I didn't know where or when another entity would appear.

I must have been seeing the array of different people for about a week when my doctor suggested that I should start to attend a support group that took place every week in the hospital. I hadn't mentioned anything about the images to him, he just thought it would do me good to attend the group and talk a little about my illness with others. At first, I didn't want to go because I knew it would be a lot of extra hassle for Fran, who would have to drive me there and back and help me in and out of the hospital. But Fran said it was no problem and that I should go.

The first meeting was on a Thursday evening so I ended up in a dayroom of the hospital with about ten other people, only two of whom were suffering with ME, the others having various other complaints. As I sat there a psychologist came in and introduced himself as the group leader and then asked the group members to introduce themselves and to say what was wrong with them. We were sitting in a circle and there was a young girl sitting opposite me who caught my eye. I looked at her and smiled but, as I did, the words 'her father is an alcoholic' flashed into my mind. I was startled. I had no idea where the words had come from; it was as if a voice had just spoken them to me. At that moment, the girl began to introduce herself. After she said her name and explained a little about her illness she said, 'One of the things really worrying me at the moment is where I will live when I leave hospital. My mother is dead and my father is an alcoholic.' I was stunned. I couldn't believe that she had said it. Then it came to my turn to introduce myself and explain what was wrong with me. But I could barely get my name out I was so shocked by what had just occurred.

Then something else happened that I couldn't explain. As I looked at the group I could see various colours begin to form around each person. I had no idea where the colours were coming from. Some of them were a dull grey and brown and they seemed to be nearly stuck to people's heads and around their shoulders, while others were a very bright red, blue and gold and they seemed to be sparking off individual people's bodies. I sat in the group feeling numb with fear. My mind began to race. 'What in the name of God is happening to me?' I asked myself. I wanted to cry.

When I got back in the car with Fran I burst into tears. Fran asked me what the matter was but all I could do was shake my head and say that I never wanted to go back to the group again. He did his best to calm me down and didn't enquire again as to what had happened. I think he felt that the whole experience of talking about my illness and listening to others do the same had been too much for me.

After the experience in the group I was truly terrified at home. I started to see the same colours that I had seen around the people in the group around the house; for no reason they would just appear in front of me. I also didn't know when one of the mysterious figures would appear again. Whatever this experience was that I was going through it was becoming more intensive and absolutely terrifying. I felt I was slowly losing control. Then, something entirely different and wonderful happened to me.

I will never forget this day for the rest of my life. It was 11 March 2001. As I lay in bed, feeling particularly drained and exhausted, I became aware of a light, pale blue, very fine energy, beginning to form in front of my bed. At first it was almost mist-like and then it began to have more substance about it and I heard a voice say, 'Don't be frightened, I'm here to help you.'

Remarkably, I didn't feel frightened. Suddenly I was at ease, and almost as if I knew I was in the company of someone who really cared for me.

'Who are you?' I asked.

'I'm an angel,' came the reply. 'A healing angel, and I'm going to help you to get better.'

The only thing I could think to say was, 'You don't look like an angel, you don't have wings.' The second I uttered the words I felt foolish. But the voice replied, 'Perhaps I don't but I'm here to help you. It won't be easy, but if you can listen and have faith in me you will recover.'

And with that the beautiful light blue energy faded away and I was left alone in my room. I reflected on what had just happened and all I wanted was for the angel to return. I had felt a sense of total ease and of being cared for during the short time she was present and I wanted that feeling back.

She had said I was going to recover from this illness. Wouldn't that be wonderful? I tried to sit up in bed but it was an effort just to prop myself up. Prior to this the only healing that I had put any faith in was that carried out by the medical profession. I remembered seeing a programme on television once about a natural healer who healed by placing his hands on people's bodies and transferring his energy to them, but I thought he was off his head to be honest.

I decided I wouldn't mention the visit from the angel to anyone. I knew telling Fran about seeing the characters in my room had just made him worry more, so I decided to keep quiet. There was also a feeling that I didn't need to tell anyone. I felt that for the moment all l needed was the help from this angel and I wished that she would re-appear.

But it was quite a while before I heard from her again. Perhaps a week went by until I looked up from my bed and there was the same pale blue energy forming in front of me.

'Where have you been?' I immediately blurted out. 'I thought you said you had come to help me?' I will never, as long as I live, forget what happened next. As I looked at the mass of energy it began to change from the top downwards and in an instant an immaculate angel, perhaps six feet tall and with the most beautiful wings I'd ever seen, was looking down at me in my bed.

I was transfixed – frozen – I couldn't do anything but stare. Eventually I said, 'I thought you didn't have wings?' Again I felt foolish, but it was all I could think to say. The angel had the most wonderful face I have ever seen; it was transparent but at the same time it had the most glorious substance. She stood at the foot of my bed radiating the most exquisite energy around the whole room. Then she said, 'Maybe seeing me like this is more helpful to you.' Her face smiled and that smile went right into me, into my soul. I felt ecstatic. Then she spoke again.

'I know your energy is very low, but we need you to begin to do certain things.' I just nodded my head and continued to gaze at her. She then began to tell me there were certain foods that I needed to stop eating, including white bread as the yeast was driving my system crazy. She also told me she wanted me to start to eat, each day, a certain type of honey I'd never heard of before. Then she mentioned certain fruits she wanted me to start eating, including kiwi fruits, which I had never tried before simply because I didn't like the look of them. She told me I would have to start eating raisins and currants every day as they were great for the blood and I was greatly lacking in iron.

She also said I had to treble my daily intake of fresh water, even though I was drinking quite a bit of water at the time. She looked at me and smiled.

'You've plenty to be getting on with,' she said. 'This is the beginning of your recovery and you'll need to be strong for what lies ahead. I will return.' And with that she was gone. But her energy wasn't gone; it still filled the room and I felt a sensation of warmth and safety, a feeling I hadn't experienced in my mind or body for a very long time.

I was now left alone and I began to think about what the angel had just told me. I trusted her totally; how couldn't I? She was a creature made of love. I just instinctively knew that. I wanted to start taking her advice immediately but I was going to need Fran's help if I was to carry out all of her requests.

It was funny to watch Fran when I tried to tell him about my new requirements. The first thing I had to do was refuse to eat the toast that he brought up to me the next morning, as it was made from white bread. I asked him to toast some wholemeal bread.

'We don't have brown wholemeal bread, you don't like it,' he replied.

I explained that I just had a sudden urge to try it and I also wanted him to get me some fruit including some kiwi fruits. He looked at me rather puzzled.

'That's a lot of fruit; you were never a big fruit fan,' he said. 'And I've never seen you eat currants or raisins before, ever.'

I then asked him to go to the health shop in the local shopping centre and get the particular honey that the angel had told me to start on.

'Honey?' he said. 'You never said you liked pure honey before. Do you like it?'

'I'm not sure, but I really want to try it,' I smiled weakly.

Fran arrived back from the shops with all the items that I asked him to get me and I began to start on my new regime. The angel had given me a lot of instructions, including leaving out potatoes and red meat from my diet. In fact, the instructions were not that hard to keep to as I had been surviving on practically nothing but soup for months now and Fran was glad when he saw that I was beginning to eat more, even if it was only fruit and honey.

Another week went by until I heard from my angel again. This time is was quite late in the evening and my room was dark when she appeared. It was as if she could adjust her energy; on this occasion, although the same pale blue colour, she wasn't as brilliant as before and her energy was more mellow, although still very beautiful and warm.

She smiled as she looked at me.

'You're doing very well, we know you don't feel it yet but you're beginning to get well,' she said softly. 'Now I want you to become aware of certain places on your body for me.'

She then moved her wing to my forehead, my throat and down just above my stomach. It was such a strange sensation; each place that she indicated to me seemed to come alive with energy, which fizzled right around my body from each of the spots the angel pointed out.

Then she said, 'These are your energy centres; people call them all sorts of different things, but that doesn't matter to us, you just become aware of them and bring your attention onto them as often as you can. It's from there that we will be healing you.' Then she asked me to do something that really surprised me.

'Downstairs you some have rocks you brought back from the beach a long time ago,' she said. I knew the rocks she was talking about. Fran, the kids and I had collected them when we were on holiday in Connemara some years before and I had three of them in our front room because I really liked them.

'I want you to put the three rocks into some water that has just been boiled with some sea salt, leave them there overnight, then have Fran bring them up to your room,' said the angel.

With that, her energy began to fade and she left the room. Again I was left alone to ponder her requests. There was something about her energy that meant when she was beside me in the room it was very easy to agree with every-thing that she was saying and very easy to believe every-thing that she said. However, once she left me I began to think about her requests. They seemed so strange that I began to have doubts. The rocks she was referring to had sat on a mantelpiece in our front room for years, what on earth could they do to help me? How was Fran going to take these requests? I didn't know, but I knew I was going to go ahead with what the angel asked, doubts or no doubts. I felt my angel was all I had at that point in time; my life-line to returning to normal health.

The next day I told Fran what I wanted him to do with the rocks. He looked at me and began to laugh.

'You want me to do what?' he said. I repeated my request.

'But why?' he asked.

'I just really like the rocks, I want them up here with me

and I want them to be clean,' I said. I could see Fran was very doubtful but he could also see that at least the rocks had stirred up some interest in me and that was something that had been sadly lacking in my personality for a long time, so he agreed to do what I asked. However, as he was leaving the room I suddenly felt that he might not do exactly what I told him to. Perhaps he would just bring the rocks up to me and not go through the whole process that the angel had spoken of.

'Fran, remember, boiled water with sea salt and leave overnight,' I said with a smile. He just nodded, smiled back and left the room.

The rocks sat on my dresser. One was oblong and very smooth, another was rather like a slate and the third was shaped like a large grey tennis ball. They had been there all day after Fran had left them in my room that morning, having done what the angel had instructed. Again, it was late in the evening when the angel appeared, her energy similar to the other evening, quite low but very warm and radiating love. She looked at the rocks and smiled.

'They're beautiful, aren't they?' she asked. I nodded.

'Yes, they are, they came from the Atlantic Ocean.' What happened next took my breath away. The angel moved over to the dresser where the rocks sat and spread her wings around the whole dresser so that the rocks and the dresser were completely enveloped by her wings. Her energy became so intensively bright that the whole dresser began to shimmer rather like a heat haze. The rocks appeared to turn nearly translucent, as if their very make-up was being altered, and I knew they were absorbing this wonderful, healing light. The angel stood for what seemed like a long time over the rocks, although it may have been only a minute. Then she spoke.

'I want you to place these rocks on the three energy spots that I pointed out to you before, just let them sit on your body at those three places, do this at least four times every day.' With that she raised her wings from around the dresser and a glorious golden energy seemed to flood the whole room as she moved. She looked down at me and said quietly, 'It takes what you refer to as time to heal. Soon you'll see what I mean and then we'll talk about what lies ahead.' Then her energy dissipated and she was gone. Again I was left alone in my room, but this time I had my rocks. It's hard to describe what I felt. After I'd witnessed what the angel had done with the rocks I knew they were going to play an important part in my healing and I felt once I had the rocks with me I had a part of the angel with me. Suddenly, after being so ill and miserable for so long, life seemed worthwhile again. I was going to get better and I was elated.

But I still had a problem: even getting out of bed was a major ordeal and I still needed Fran to help me with the job of getting the rocks onto my energy spots as the angel had instructed me. I was still nervous about telling Fran about the angel. I was afraid for him – I thought he'd really become frightened for me and I didn't know what he might do. But I also made up my mind that once I was feeling better and it was obvious that I was getting well I would tell Fran everything about the angel.

What was really miraculous was that I knew I was going to get better. At that point I knew I would recover; I had no doubts, and it was a mighty realisation.

The next day, when Fran came up with my breakfast, I

said I needed to talk with him. I asked him how he felt about the rocks that were sitting on my dresser.

'How do I feel about them?' he asked, frowning slightly.

'Yes. I really like them, do you like them?'

'I've always liked them, ever since we collected them,' he said. 'Why do you ask?'

'Because I need you to trust me here, Fran,' I said.

'To trust you? You know I trust you,' he replied.

'Yes I do, but I need you to do something for me without asking any questions and I promise I'll explain everything to you in due course,' I said. I then told him what I wanted him to do with the rocks and to my surprise he just agreed.

'I don't know what it is about those rocks,' he said, 'but they've managed to instil some life in you that I haven't seen in a long time, so I'll do what you say.'

And so we began. Fran would put the rocks on my energy spots first thing in the morning, then around midday, then late in the afternoon and then last thing at night. He would leave them there for about half an hour. For the first three days I didn't notice any difference, and if anything I began to feel worse on the second day. But on the fourth day, after the mid-day session, I began to feel a tingling. It started first around my stomach area where the rock was lying, and after that I was quickly aware of energy flowing through all the spots where the rocks were positioned. I was overjoyed, but it wasn't a constant and on other days I'd feel absolutely nothing at all.

Then the angel appeared to me again. It had been perhaps two weeks since I'd heard from her and I was delighted when I looked up and saw that beautiful pale blue energy.

'You've done really well,' she said. 'We're all really pleased with you, but now we need you take a step further. I want you to get up out of your bed and begin to walk.'

When she spoke the words I had the sudden urge to burst out crying. It had been so long since I had walked without being helped around by Fran, and I felt that it was all too much for me to take. I was scared and I felt I'd fail. 'Little steps, that's all we're asking, even out to your front gate, we know you can do it,' smiled the angel.

Now the gate she was referring to was about thirty feet from my front door but it could have been thirty miles because I had hardly been downstairs in my house for the last four months and then Fran had to help me. I started to cry again; this time I bawled, I was terrified.

'We know you can do it,' said the angel, and disappeared.

The next day I said to Fran, 'I want you to help me downstairs, carry me if you have to, I'm going to try and walk out to the front gate.' I was surprised when he simply said, 'Good let's do it.'

It turned out that Fran didn't have to carry me, but I did need to hold on to him and let him basically drag me along. When we got to our front door he said, 'Are you sure you want to try for the front gate?' I nodded, but I was trembling, it seemed such a long way away. But we made it and we made it back again. I was overcome with emotion; I couldn't believe that I had managed it. But it really took its toll and when we got back into the house I said, 'There's no way I can make it back up those stairs. I feel like someone has just beaten me up, I'm going to sleep on the settee tonight.'

And that's what I did, not only that night but for the

next week, as Fran and I made the trip from our front door out to our front gate more and more often. The day I made the journey out to the front gate and back by myself was a joyous day. I hugged Fran and we both laughed and laughed, it seemed so important. It was now late May 2001, nearly eighteen months since I had first been diagnosed with ME.

It wasn't long before I was making my way, on my own, up to the corner of our estate, perhaps 100 metres away, and back to the house. And so it continued, small distances gradually became bigger distances until I was able to take a walk by myself to the end of our estate, where it met with the main road, a distance of perhaps a quarter of a mile. It was after about two months of this gradual recovery that I decided the time was right to tell Fran about the angel. He had seen the progress I had made and even before I told him I sensed that he knew something was helping me to make this remarkable turnaround.

'I need to tell you something,' I said to him one evening as we sat in our front room. 'You remember when I told you that those characters were appearing to me in my room a while ago?' I asked.

'Yes,' he replied.

'Well that was the truth, they really did appear and after that an angel appeared to me and told me how to get well. That's why I asked you to get me the fruit and the honey and it's also why I asked you to bring the rocks to my room and put them on my energy spots.' He looked bewildered.

'Well ... it's wonderful that your energy is returning and that you're beginning to feel well again, really wonderful,'

he uttered. I could see and feel that he wanted to understand it all, but it was a bit too much for him. The next
day, Fran had gone to work and I was alone in my room
when the angel appeared.

'You've done so well; we're so pleased with you,' she
said.

'Yes, but my husband thinks I'm completely insane,' I
replied.

'You leave Fran to us; we're going to give him a sign,'
smiled the angel. I looked at her; she was radiant, majestic,
the whole room filled with a sense of lightness and deep
peace.

'Why do you always say "us" or "we" in the plural?' I
asked.

'Because you're dealing with the angelic realm, there's a
great many of us,' came the reply.

# 3

## A Very Special Gift

It was such a joyous feeling to be back up on my feet and to start to do normal things with my family again. Simple things like going for a walk or just being able to sit and watch a programme on television with Fran and the boys – all these things seemed new to me, as if I had never done any of them before. I was really able to appreciate them and I realised that the simple things in life were truly good.

What was also very good was the fact that my healing angel, who had played such a huge role in my recovery, was still very much around me. Maybe it was remiss of me, but up to this point I had never thought to ask her what her name was. I didn't even know if angels had names like human beings do. So I asked her. To my surprise she answered simply, 'My name is Anne.'

I was delighted – my angel had a name, Anne. I could now call her Angel Anne. I don't know why I felt so happy to hear her name; perhaps it was because I felt if I knew her name it would be easier for me to call her and to keep in contact with her and that was what I wanted to do more than anything else. Angel Anne was now appearing several times a week and one day, while I sat on my settee in our front room, she materialised and said, 'The time has come for you to learn a very important part of your work with us. We're going to teach you how to channel.'

I asked her what she meant by channel. She replied, 'At the moment you can hear and see me because we bring ourselves to you, but you must learn how to be able to call the angel realm and the spirit world whenever you wish. It's known as being able to channel.'

I was very surprised, but also excited, by this news. The thought that I could actually call an angel to me whenever I needed one was an amazing idea, but it was also a very humbling thought. I started to have doubts.

'I don't really know if I deserve to have that kind of ability,' I said hesitantly. Angel Anne smiled and said softly, 'You leave it up to us to decide if you deserve it or not.' And then she told me to do something odd.

'There's a *Yellow Pages* telephone book in your kitchen; I want you to go and get it and open it at any page that you choose.' I went into the kitchen and picked up the *Yellow Pages* and returned to the front room. Sitting down, I opened the book at roughly halfway through. Looking straight at me was an advertisement for an establishment advertising complementary medicine on the south side of Dublin. I immediately knew that what Angel Anne had told me about channelling was relevant to this establishment, although I had absolutely no idea about what went on there.

I noticed that the advertisement mentioned several courses, I suppose you could call them new-age courses, that took place regularly at this Centre. Then Angel Anne spoke again.

'We want you to go on a course there, it's very important

that you do.' Immediately I was filled with doubts. Here I was, an ordinary housewife, still in the early stages of recovery from a serious illness and now I was being asked to attend a course I had no interest in and knew absolutely nothing about.

'But I can't just turn up at this place,' I said. 'I wouldn't know anyone there. I don't have a clue about any of the courses and it's miles away on the south side.' I must have sounded quite desperate because Angel Anne smiled and said, 'Remember, it's faith that has you up and walking around now, just have a little faith in what we're asking you to do, all will be well.'

So I took up the phone and dialled the number of the centre. A woman's voice answered the phone. She didn't sound as if she was from Ireland, but she was very nice and told me that there were only two places left on a course to do with the human aura, so I booked myself in, even though I only had a very vague idea what the human aura actually was at that stage.

The courses were short, just two afternoons each weekend and the one I booked began on the coming Saturday and Sunday. So, on the Saturday, Fran took me across town to the south side. I looked at the building before I entered – it was a rather old, red-brick place and I got the impression that several businesses possibly operated from it. As I went in there was a notice board that indicated the various activities that went on there. The board directed me to the second floor where the Centre was based. A girl sitting behind a desk directed me into a large room with whitewashed walls. There were a number of chairs positioned in rows and some big cushions lay around on the floor. I made my way shyly into the room. Already there were about ten people present and, of course, I didn't know anyone and I was feeling very unsure of myself. 'What in the name of God am I doing here?' I asked myself. These people obviously knew why they were all here and had probably done similar courses before. I feared I was among a group who somehow led an alternative lifestyle and were very interested in things like yoga and natural healing, things I really knew nothing about.

While my life prior to getting ill had been very happy, it was largely consumed with rearing my children, which entailed doing the school run in the mornings and after-noons, helping with their homework in the evenings and attending football matches or taking them swimming at the weekends. I was happy, but looking back now, perhaps I was also a little under-confident and I had settled into a rather dull routine without really becoming aware of it. However, I was very aware of how uncertain I felt about myself standing in this room surrounded by so many strangers.

One girl with short blonde hair caught my eye; she was much younger then me.

'Hi, I'm Jean,' she introduced herself. I held out my hand and smiled.

'I'm Penny,' I said and at once felt a little better; at least I was talking to someone. Jean then proceeded to tell me that she was very interested in yoga and hoped one day to become an instructor. She was also very interested in the human aura and this was not the first time she had taken a course on the subject. This only served to confirm for me that the room was full of people who knew exactly why they were here and what they wanted to achieve by being here. I felt even more lost and out of place.

Eventually, a lovely looking woman, aged I would guess in her mid-fifties, came into the room. She wasn't Irish and I wasn't sure where exactly she was from; her skin was a lovely soft brown, and she looked possibly Mexican or Brazilian to me. She addressed the group and told us her name was Emmy-Lou and that she was going to present the course on the human aura.

There was a large flip board behind her with some pages that seemed to contain an outline of the human body; around the outline were very bright colours of different intensities. Emmy-Lou began to explain how the aura was an energy field that basically emanates from the body and some people could actually see other people's auras. She continued with her lecture for about twenty minutes and I found it interesting but a little bit beyond my comprehension. Then she said we were going to do an exercise to see if we could determine where our auras actually were. She teamed everyone up with a partner, but there was an uneven number of people present so she said I could work with her for the purpose of the exercise.

The first thing we had to do was to sit opposite each other and try to focus in on each other's auras. I began to concentrate on the area around Emmy-Lou's head, but something happened that made me nearly jump off my seat. As I sat looking at her, from nowhere a very large Native American Indian appeared right behind her. He didn't look quite like an Indian you would see in a cowboy film on television; his skin was very brown and his hair was jet black and while he had what looked like traditional

Indian clothes on, made from leather or cowhide, he also wore what looked like some modern clothes. He must have been over six feet in height and was a very impressive sight. He gazed at Emmy-Lou – it was a proud loving look, as if he was really interested in her and also very pleased with her.

Emmy-Lou began to speak to the group again and the sight of the Indian faded away behind her. I didn't know what to do. I was startled because it had happened so suddenly and unexpectedly. Emmy-Lou then asked the group to begin another exercise. This time we had to stand up and face each other, about 20 feet apart, then we were to slowly walk towards each other and try to physically feel where our energy fields began. By this stage I wasn't really taking it all in, all I could think about was the amazing sight I had just witnessed. As I got closer to Emmy-Lou it happened again. This time more Native American Indians appeared from nowhere in a scene that looked to be from an Indian reservation. There was the same Indian man but this time a woman was with him and beside them was what looked like a wolf. Again, they just smiled and seemed to converse with each other before turning their loving gaze onto Emmy-Lou. I was completely confused. Here I was, trying to take in what was being said about our auras and energy fields, while at the same time I was witnessing these amazing scenes apparently from an Indian reservation. Why was this happening to me? Who were these people? What did they want? I didn't know the answer to any of these questions, but I had a strong sense that Emmy-Lou held the answers.

After another two exercises, Emmy-Lou wound up the

session, thanked the group and said she would see us all the next day. Slowly, everyone filtered out of the room but as I was passing Emmy-Lou I stopped and said to her, 'Do you mind if I ask you something?' 'Not at all,' she smiled. 'Have you any connection with Native American Indians?' I asked. She looked quizzically at me and said, 'Yes, I'm descended from the Native Indians, how did you know?' I then explained to her about what had happened during the course of the afternoon and what I had witnessed. She smiled broadly when I told her about the two Indians appearing, and the wolf.

'That wasn't a wolf,' she said. 'That was Sabre. He was my grandfather's dog and the two people you are describing are my grandfather and grandmother; they raised me on an Indian reservation in Alaska.' I was stunned, all I could think to say was, 'Why are they appearing to me, do they want something?' Emmy-Lou smiled at me and touched my arm.

'I don't think they want anything except to let me know that they love me and that they are there for me,' she replied. But then she said something else that really surprised me.

'You're very gifted, you've been given the gift of being able to communicate with the spirit world and you're the first person I've ever met who was able to reach my grandparents, besides myself. You have a wonderful ability to channel.'

Emmy-Lou then asked me to come downstairs with her to have a cup of coffee. We made our way down to a small kitchen that was obviously used by the people who worked in the building, but there was no one else there and we sat down. I suddenly felt very at ease with

Emmy-Lou and I decided to tell her the reason that I was taking the course.

She sat and listened intently as I explained about my illness, about Angel Anne appearing to me and my gradual recovery. Then I told her about opening the *Yellow Pages* at exactly the page the advertisement for the centre was on and Angel Anne telling me to come on the course to learn to channel.

'Wow, that's an amazing story,' she said after I'd finished. 'You've been given a very special gift. I feel it's not a course on the human aura you should be taking, but a course in meditation. I asked her why and she said, 'Well you'll find that if you can meditate and become still it will be that much easier to reach your angels and the spirit world.'

Suddenly it all began to make more sense to me. Every time Angel Anne had appeared to me it was a truly wonderful experience, but then I had to return to the everyday world with all its comings and goings and I didn't like it one bit. I felt restless and I longed for the times when Angel Anne would reappear. But now, here was Emmy-Lou telling me that all I needed to do was to learn to relax and be still, not only for myself, but in order to contact the angel realm and the spirit world when I wanted to. I didn't need to be told twice – I was going to learn to meditate properly.

The day following the course Angel Anne appeared to me at home.

'You did so well at the course; we're all so pleased with you,' she said. 'You're ability to channel will become stronger and clearer the more you actually do it,' she explained. 'What Emmy-Lou suggested about meditation was correct but I also want you to know that meditation is a simple process; it's simply the ability to quiet your mind, and when your mind is quiet you will find it so much easier to communicate with us. I'm going to take you through a simple meditation now if you don't mind.' That last sentence proved to be a massive understatement.

Angel Anne told me to relax and imagine I was sitting by a lovely river on a beautiful day and the river was gently flowing past me. Then she told me to imagine that the river was actually taking me to a place of great peace within myself. As I went further and further into that place of perfect peace Angel Anne's energy seemed to grow dim, so much so that I was afraid she was going to vanish but then her beautiful light blue energy began to slowly throb and grow brighter.

It grew brighter and brighter until it began to pulsate with such an intensity that I felt it was too much, as if I couldn't bear it, but I somehow knew that I needed to stay focused. It was as if some type of adjustment then took place within my own energy; it seemed to blend with Angel Anne's and I was able to continue looking at her. She smiled at me and I felt elated.

'Welcome home,' she said.

'Home?' I said. 'Am I home?'

'Yes, welcome to the angel realm. You've done so well, we're very proud of you,' she replied.

Then I began to discern another colour come into her wondrous pale blue, light body. This time it was a beautiful shade of green; it shimmered and seemed to concentrate itself around her left shoulder. Then a shade of absolutely glorious magenta began to pulsate around her head. She stood in front of me and radiated divinity.

'Your colours,' I said. 'They're different, there's many more of them.' Even as I was speaking I could see new shades of the most amazingly intense colours beginning to form in different parts of her light body. They began to get so intense that I felt the need to look away. I could feel tears begin to well up in my eyes. It was as if I wasn't worthy of seeing what was taking place in front of me.

'It's all right, be still, be still,' soothed Angel Anne. 'When you look into my colours you look into the angel realm. I said before there are a great many of us, so there are a great many colours.'

Something truly incredible then began to happen. As I looked in wonder at the beautiful colours they began to take shape as individual angels. I looked at the green I had seen at Angel Anne's shoulder and a tall male angel began to materialise; his colours seemed to alternate between green and shades of light pink throughout. When I say a male angel began to materialise I've come to understand that angels actually don't have any gender, but they will appear to someone as male or female depending on that person's actual perception of the angel they are communicating with and this angel taking form in front of me was that of a tall man who had the most caring face I'd ever seen. His eyes were soft and they shone love. Then Angel Anne spoke, 'This is the Archangel Raphael, God's servant. He is here to help anyone who suffers with pain, especially if you hold on to past pain or trauma, or if you are under any kind of medical supervision, Archangel Raphael is here to help you. All you need do is call upon him.' The archangel then faded back into Angel Anne's light body.

Then my gaze was drawn to the deep shade of magenta I'd seen around Angel Anne's head and another wonderful angel took shape in front of me. This time he was a much slighter figure and his face was full of fun. It was as if he really wanted to tell me a joke but the time wasn't quite right; his eyes twinkled and danced.

'This is the Archangel Gabriel,' said Angel Anne. 'He is a wonderful angel of direction, or if you need more humour and laughter in your life he's there for you, or if you're planing to have a family and need some advice he's at your call.'

Then another angel took shape in front of me. He had a mighty presence about him, very solid, and he carried within him a great sense of authority. His colours shone with a brilliant white and flashes of gold seemed to spark around him. Even Angel Anne's voice seemed to change to a tone of respect as she introduced him.

'This is the Archangel Michael, the carrier of God's sword of justice and flame of light,' she said, as if she too was in awe of him. 'Michael is always there for those of you who feel lost or hopeless. Maybe you have problems with drink or drugs and the world has abandoned you; if so, turn to Archangel Michael and ask that his sword of protection be directed towards you and your worldly problems will melt.'

Around Angel Anne's feet was a lovely hue of yellow, and as I gazed at it an angel smaller than any of the others appeared.

'This is the Archangel Uriel,' said Angel Anne. 'If you

get bored or distracted with life very easily you can call on Uriel. If you feel you're drifting or constantly at a cross-roads in life, he will bring the presence of God's love and serenity into your life.'

As I continued to look at Angel Anne I noticed that her colours were now returning to her original pale blue. She looked at me and said, 'There are many more angels and in time you will come to know them and to work with them. Each one of them has the ability to help and guide people in all areas of their daily lives. They only want to bring joy, peace, love, prosperity and abundance into people's lives, but remember, all the angel realm consists of is the love of God already dwelling inside each and every one of you. Go now and start our work.'

With that, her energy began to dissipate and she slowly disappeared but I knew somewhere deep inside of me that what had been revealed to me was just the beginning of a long journey that I was about to take – the angels and I.

# 4

## Mountain of Change

I decided to legally change my name by deed poll three years ago, from Penelope Gibbs to Francesca Brown. It was not a decision taken lightly and it caused quite a lot of turmoil and upset, not so much for myself but for my family and extended family.

I am about to explain the reasons why I did this and they may appear quite fantastic to many people reading this book. However, at the end of the day, for me it was simply a case of doing what the angels asked of me, and as usual they were absolutely right.

When we moved to Blanchardstown some of the first people we made friends with were a lovely young couple, Kieran and Catherine, who lived next door to us. They were great neighbours and we really became very friendly with them in a short space of time. As you can imagine we were delighted when they told us of their plans to get married and even more delighted when they invited us to the wedding in August 2001. The wedding was to be in Letterkenny, County Donegal, as Kieran was originally from Northern Ireland. It was to take place on a Saturday so Fran and I decided we would travel to Donegal on the Friday and return to Dublin on the following Monday.

We started off early that Friday morning, as the trip to

Donegal was a long one by car. My energy was getting stronger and stronger as the days went by, and I was feeling happy and looking forward to the weekend that lay ahead of us.

We had been travelling for perhaps a couple of hours when suddenly the image of a mountain flashed into my mind. It was a very vivid image and I could see the area in great detail. By this time I had begun to realise that when the angels gave me an image of anything there was a purpose to it, so I paid great attention to the scene in front of me. I could see a pathway that led up and appeared to go over the mountain. I had the sense that a great many people had travelled this pathway. The mountain scene was very beautiful, but there was also a sense of sadness about the place. The image of the mountain eventually faded away but I was left with a very strong feeling that it was important and I would be seeing it again. I told Fran about what I'd seen and he said that it could be one of the mountains around Donegal and perhaps I was just seeing somewhere we were going to end up visiting during the weekend. But I knew that the mountain held a far greater significance than that.

When we eventually reached Donegal we booked into our hotel and Fran decided he would go for a walk to stretch his legs. I said I'd stay in the room and maybe take a nap. I had just lain down on the bed when the image of the mountain reappeared in my consciousness. This time it was even more vivid; I could see people moving along the pathway and then a voice in my head uttered these words, 'This is a place of loss and of great change.' That's all the voice said and with that the image faded. But I was now determined to find out more about this mountain and why it seemed to be of such importance to the angels.

That evening, Fran and I had dinner in the hotel dining room and then decided we would visit a pub in the town for a drink. I had told Fran about seeing the mountain again and that it somehow seemed to be very important that I find more information about it. So, when he was up ordering drinks he asked the barman if there were any mountains nearby.

'Mountains?' he replied. 'The only mountain around here worth seeing is Muckish.' The instant Fran said the name Muckish to me I knew that it was the mountain I'd seen and that I had to visit it.

The next day we enjoyed the lovely wedding of Kieran and Catherine. It was a beautiful ceremony, and it looked as if it would turn into a very late night when I turned to Fran and said, 'I think it's time for us to head to our bed. I want to be up and ready to go in the morning to find out more about Muckish.'

There was a slight drizzle coming down as we pointed the car towards the mountain the next morning. As we drove through the country roads I suddenly became aware of a feeling of great expectation, of what I didn't exactly know, but I knew that I was exactly where I was supposed to be at that moment.

As we turned a corner, the mountain came into view. It stood in front of us as if it were guarding something and was careful about who it admitted into its secret. As we stood at its base I could see the same pathway that I had witnessed earlier; it crept up and over the mountain. Slowly we began to walk up until we got onto the actual pathway that leads up the mountainside. At one point, not quite halfway up the slope, we came to a statue of the Blessed Virgin. There was an old man sitting on a little wall close by.

'Be very careful as you climb, it's very slippery today,' he cautioned. We nodded in agreement and continued on our way. As we progressed the mountain dipped a little and opened up into a small valley. Suddenly I had a total change of consciousness. Everything changed. It was as if the whole valley took on a different dimension, everything became alive, totally alive. Everything in an instant was made immaculately whole – that's the only way I can describe it. It happened in a flash – quicker than that. I could actually hear the grass growing; I could sense all the small animals around me on the mountain; birds flew past and it was as if I was with them in flight. I had the very strange experience of understanding that I was made from the same essence as the grass, the sky, the mountain and everything on it. I suddenly understood the real meaning of God's world. It is one. It is made from God although there are many animals and people and things in it, it is already perfectly whole – there is only God appearing as animals and people and things. All is one. This revelation stunned me. It made me feel totally insignificant as a person; in fact I disappeared there and then.

I turned to try and speak to Fran, but I couldn't; what I was experiencing was beyond words, words couldn't possibly describe it. Everything just seemed to be sitting perfectly in this vast, vast space; everything was just sitting there in divine order as God intended. It was immaculate.

I somehow knew that we should continue climbing, so

we walked on until we could see a little clearing up ahead of us. I told Fran I was going to go ahead and sit down, as I wanted to stop and try to take in everything that was happening to me. But I didn't have time to sit down.

Out of nowhere a lady wearing what looked like rather old but good country tweeds appeared in the clearing in front of me. I knew she was an angel although I had never seen her before. She radiated kindness, although she looked rather solemn. I looked closer at what she was wearing; she had a sort of cape made from tweed slung from her shoulder down to around her waist, a large brooch held it in place on her shoulder. She wore a skirt made from rough tweed and she had open sandals on that were tied with leather twine up past her ankles. Although her clothes were quite rough-looking there was a certain quality to them and she had an authority about her as if this was her place and she was very much at home. Then she spoke.

'This is a place of loss and of great change.' The same words I had heard uttered earlier in my hotel room. I couldn't think of what to say so I said, 'Why have you brought me here?'

'All of us must give,' she replied. 'Now the time has come for you to give us your name.' I looked at her, puzzled – give them my name, what could she mean?

'I don't understand; you want me to give you my name?' I said.

'Yes, you are no longer Penelope Gibbs. From now on you must become Francesca Brown,' she replied.

'Francesca Brown?' I said, puzzled. 'I've never heard of her, why would I change my name to that? Is she someone I'm going to meet?'

'Penelope Gibbs is dead; you were always Francesca Brown,' came the reply. 'While you were ill your soul was crying out to go home and God heard your cries so he took your soul. But your journey wasn't finished here on earth; you still had work to do, so you returned but from now on you will be known as Francesca Brown. She is your true identity and it is through her that you will do our work here on earth.'

'But I didn't die; my soul never left me,' I said, still confused.

'Everything happens for a reason. God has many ways; your soul did leave you and you are now Francesca Brown. Have faith; all is well,' replied the angel. She looked at me and smiled. I could feel her loving energy fill me, but before I could say anything else her energy began to fade away, leaving me alone on the mountainside and still quite a distance away from Fran.

I sat down on a big rock nearby. I realised I was trembling and I was totally confused. Could it be true? Did my soul actually leave me during my illness? It certainly felt as if everything had left me at one stage; all my energy was gone but I never actually lost the will to live and I never had any real acknowledgement that God was even interested in my life until Angel Anne appeared to me. Yet this experience had just happened to me, this angel seemed certain that I now had a new identity – that of someone called Francesca Brown. Then Fran came up to where I was sitting.

'Are you alright? You were just staring at that spot for a long time,' he said, pointing to where the angel had appeared.

'I don't know,' I replied. 'Something very strange has just happened to me. I'll tell you about it later.' I felt I couldn't even begin to explain to him what had just taken place.

A slightly heavier drizzle had now begun to fall on the mountainside and I knew that we should start to descend from where we were. It had been quite hard climbing up this far and the surface was now becoming more slippery, yet I didn't want to leave the place, it was as if I needed to find out more before we left.

However, Fran insisted that we begin to make our way down the mountain, so we slowly began to descend, taking great care as the slope was now well and truly wet. When we eventually made it back to the spot where the statue of the Blessed Virgin was, the old man we had seen on our way up was still there and he greeted us.

'Did you have a nice walk?' he enquired.

'Yes we did,' I replied. 'It's a lovely mountain. Are you from around here?'

'Indeed I am, and my father before me and his father before him,' he said with a laugh.

'Do you have any idea why this mountain would be called a place of loss and of great change?' I asked.

'Well, of course I do,' he said. 'A great many people who were leaving for America and Australia during the famine years would have had to cross over this mountain from Donegal to get to the port of Derry.' Then he pointed to a small bridge we had seen earlier and said, 'That bridge is known as "The Bridge Of Sorrows", so many people stood on that bridge and when they looked behind them they could see the village they were leaving and their loved ones. They'd turn and wave and their loved ones would wave back, then they would take another few steps and be gone forever, gone into a new world.'

As he spoke I felt the tears welling up inside me; I could feel all those people's loss all those years ago, the sadness must have been nearly unbearable. I now understood why I was brought here – it was indeed a place of loss and of great change and I was now being asked to make a change. I was being asked to give up something. Just like those emigrants so many years ago had to give up something very dear to them to make way for the new, I too was being asked to give up something very precious to me so the new could come and begin its work.

We thanked the old man and shook hands with him. He took my hand in a firm grip and said, 'What is your name, Ma'am, if you don't mind me asking?'

'It's Francesca,' I replied. 'Francesca Brown.'

But if I thought that the experience on the side of Muckish was the only surprise the angels had in store for me that day I was very wrong.

Fran and I decided we would take a different route back to our hotel, as it was still quite early in the afternoon. We drove until we came to a beautiful beach, where we stopped the car and decided to take a short walk. As we were walking I began to try and explain to Fran what had taken place on the mountainside and that the angel had asked me to change my name. He looked really worried as I related the exact details of what the angel had asked me to do.

'What will we tell the kids, your family, my family?' he said anxiously. 'They're going to think that it's all very weird and strange.'

'I don't think it has to happen all at once, we can take our time and plan it,' I said. Then I remembered what the angel had told me and I said, 'Have faith. God has many ways.'

As we left the beach and started to drive back towards our hotel we came upon another hotel. The evening was beginning to draw in and its lights twinkled in the gathering dusk.

'Let's stop and have a drink,' suggested Fran. I think he felt that we both needed one after what had just happened on the mountainside! I agreed, so we drove the car up a long winding driveway that led to the hotel. Then something totally remarkable happened. As I looked at the car park in front of the hotel, where there were a lot of coaches and some cars parked, I became aware of five or six angels standing behind individual people who were all going into the hotel. At once I thought these must be those people's guardian angels, because they kept so close to them and they seemed to be interested only in them. It was as if they were lovingly shadowing them.

I will never forget what happened next as long as I live. As we entered the hotel there were angels literally everywhere, the whole building was lit up with their wondrous light bodies. The sight overwhelmed me and I couldn't keep my attention from them, there seemed to be literally dozens of angels. We made our way into the lounge and ordered drinks. As people entered the lounge their angel would be right behind or beside them and all the time the angels seemed to be totally engrossed with each particular person.

Eventually all the people left the lounge and the room

seemed to dim as the amazing energy emanating from the angels left with the people. But something else had caught my eye: although each and every angel shone with an absolutely brilliant light, some of the people they were shadowing did not look very well, in fact one or two of them seemed to be very ill-looking indeed.

We could hear music coming from somewhere out in the hotel; it sounded like a live band was playing and I recognised one of the songs as I used to dance to it years ago. After a while I got up to go to the bathroom and as I was coming back the music was really loud and seemed to be coming from a room to the side of the lounge. I couldn't resist it; I just had to have a look inside the room.

What I saw when I opened the door made me stop in my tracks. There were angels everywhere; their presence was so bright it made the entire room light up like a big wonderful kaleidoscope of loving energy. As people got up and danced with each other the angels seemed to be overjoyed and I could see some of them behind people trying to encourage them to get up and dance; it was a joyous and really vibrant sight. I suddenly had an overwhelming urge to join the dancing so I went back into the lounge and asked Fran if he would come and join me in the room for a dance.

'But we can't just go in and start dancing, we don't know anyone,' he protested.

'I've a feeling it will be alright, just trust me,' I replied and pulled him up from his seat. As we entered the room a couple were dancing in front of us and they immediately made room for us as if inviting us to dance. The band was playing another tune – a great song to dance to – and Fran and I really began to enjoy ourselves as we danced away with all these lovely people – and possibly as many as forty angels! We stayed dancing for another three songs until we began to feel a little tired and we sat down at a line of chairs that were positioned along the side of the room. Then two girls, perhaps in their late twenties came and sat down beside us.

'Everyone is having a wonderful time,' I said to one of them.

'Yes,' she replied. 'Did you come up with the group from Galway or Dublin?' I had to tell her the truth – that Fran and I had just stolen into their party because it seemed so much fun. She laughed out loud and said, 'Well you're very welcome; it's great to get up and have a dance, it's good for the soul.' I agreed with her and thanked her for her hospitality.

We then decided it was time for us to be making our way back to our hotel in time for our evening meal. But as we were walking through the hotel car park to our car something caught my attention. There was a big white coach parked close to our car and on it in red letters was the name of a big cancer hospital in Dublin and on another coach I noticed the name of a well-known cancer support group. Then it dawned on me. All the people back in the hotel were suffering with different stages of cancer and their guardian angels were there with them supporting them through what must have been the most difficult period of their lives.

As we drove that road back to our hotel in Letterkenny I felt so honoured and humbled by these amazing people, their spirit and their energy. I also felt very comforted by the knowledge that their guardian angels were there for them. I wanted to turn the car back and to tell each and every one of them this great truth, that their angels were there by their sides, but I somehow knew that it wasn't my place to do that just then.

# 5

## The Spirit Guides

People have often asked me what the difference is between a spirit guide and an angel. Well, a spirit guide is the evolved spirit of someone who has passed from this earth and returns to assist human beings in their life's journey while still here on earth. Some spirit guides tend to be highly evolved beings that can bring enormous comfort to people during their lives, while others are less evolved and their purpose in the spirit world can be less clear. People who can contact spirit guides are sometimes referred to as 'mediums' or 'clairvoyants'.

An angel is a celestial being of light sent by God. However, the work carried out by spirit guides and angels is entirely different. Some spirit guides can be a great comfort to those of us living on earth but an angel can actually help us to become closer to God; they are God's messengers and their light is in fact the light of God.

I have many spirit guides who contact me on a regular basis. One of them is a black American gentleman called Eamon. When he first appeared to me he told me that I had a great gift and that I could bring a lot of happiness and comfort to people and that he'd like to work with me, so I agreed. Eamon is a constant source of good humour and positive energy and he has a great sense of feeling and concern for those of us who have just lost a loved one here on earth. I've had many lovely positive encounters with beings from the spirit world and it is all down to Eamon's guidance and help.

One encounter involving Eamon will stay with me for a long time simply because it was so lovely. An elderly lady came to see me. Her son brought her to my front door; she was in her seventies and she looked quite old and sad. As we began to chat, Eamon suddenly appeared to me and said, 'I have someone here who really wants to say hello to this lady.' With that, a tall, handsome man appeared and stood beside the lady. He knew everything about her and he talked about when they were courting and then about their married life.

'Tell her I love her and that I lie down beside her in bed every night before she goes to sleep,' he said. The lady began to cry and she said that she could feel his presence beside her each night. Then the man related many of the couple's favourite pieces of music that they used to dance to and places that they used to frequent.

'Tell her that I've never forgotten her, in fact I was never farther than a hair's breadth away from her in all the years since we've parted,' said the man with a lovingly gentle smile. 'But tell her that I have to go now because my liver and onions are on the table and they'll get cold.'

So I related what the man had said and, sure enough, the lady confirmed to me that liver and onions were this man's favourite meal – he used to have it at least twice a week. It was such a touching scene that the lady and I both cried a little, then we laughed and chatted for a while. Then the lady rang her son to come and collect her. When he arrived he said, 'My God, what have you done with my mother? She looks twenty years younger than when I left her with you a little while ago!'

That was very typical of the kind of work that Eamon can do and he's tireless, always up and on the go, trying to help in any way that he can. But Eamon also has a very practical side to him. A lady who, I would guess, was in her late twenties once came to see me. She had a young daughter but was separated from the child's father and she seemed to be quite unhappy with her life. She explained that things were difficult for her at the moment in time: she was working in a job that she didn't like but had to keep it up to support her child and she felt quite lonely most of the time.

Then Eamon came on the scene. He said he had the young lady's grandfather there with him and he wanted to communicate with his granddaughter. Although I couldn't actually see the grandfather he had a lot of advice for his granddaughter, which he relayed through Eamon.

'Tell her that she should be flying, that's what she always wanted to do and she can do it,' he said. I asked the young lady if she understood the statement that she should be flying. She looked at me in amazement and said, 'Well, yes, I've always wanted to be an air hostess but I just never seemed to get the chance to go and do it.'

'Tell her she can do it. I know she can do it, and tell her that her family will support her if she just asks them,' said her grandfather. Then Eamon gave me the name Betty. He told me this woman was very important to the young woman with me and would play an important role in her life in years to come. So I asked her if the name meant anything to her.

'Well, I have an auntie named Betty, whom I'm very close to. She's very good to me and my daughter,' replied the young woman. We chatted a little more and then she took her leave of me. I didn't see her again for eighteen months, then one day I was shopping in the local super-market when I ran into her with her little daughter. She beamed at me and said, 'I want to thank you. After I left you I resolved I was going to go after my dream and I applied for the position of air hostess and I got the job. It hasn't been easy but I'm happier now than at any other time in my life and my family are a great support, including my auntie Betty, who looks after my daughter a lot when I'm out working. I'm flying high, thank you. Thank my grandfather and especially thank Eamon.'

Eamon has been responsible for introducing me to lot of very special people; his energy never fails to amaze me. He also seems to have the ability to reach the spirits of a great many people who have passed into the light, no matter what dimension or plane they inhabit in the spirit world. However, he did surprise me when I awoke one night in my bedroom in Dublin to find him looking down on me.

'What do you want at this time of the night?' I asked him.

'I've someone very special here who wants to meet with you,' he replied. I got up and sat on the edge of my bed. Suddenly, the whole room was enveloped in a very lovely gentle light; it was as if the atmosphere of an early summer's day had been transported into my room and I realised I could smell a beautiful fresh scent. Suddenly I was filled with a sense of deep peace and of gentle expectancy.

As I looked out at the dark, a young woman dressed as

a Carmelite nun appeared in front of me. There was a most glorious presence and sense of calm and peace about her. I asked her name.

'My name is Thérèse, Saint Thérèse of Lisieux,' she replied. I noticed that at her feet was a small mound of reddish-brown clay and a jug filled with water. She bent down and began to rub some of the clay onto my feet and then she poured water from the jug over them until they were clean. She did this with both feet and then she smiled the most wondrously sweet smile at me. I felt mesmerised.

'Why did you just do that to my feet?' I asked her.

'So that you may go more lightly in your work,' she replied. She stood above me for a little while smiling and then her image slowly began to fade from the room.

This young woman's presence stayed with me for a long time after she had disappeared. It's difficult to describe in words the effect that she had on me. I felt fortified, as if I had been given a hidden strength, whose power lay in compassion and gentleness and service to that which is good.

It was not the only time I was to be visited by St Thérèse, however. Some four years later she appeared to me again, this time it was in a small town called Orihuela Costa, close to Alicante in southern Spain. I was sitting on a deckchair enjoying the sun when I casually reached over and picked up a book by a well-known spiritual writer, a book that I had been browsing through for the past few days. For no particular reason I opened the book at a certain page and there before me were the words 'Saint Thérèse of Lisieux'. I immediately felt the same sensation of deep peace over-come me as I had experienced before in my bedroom. I was sitting on a sunroof at the time and as I looked at the wall opposite me I began to see the image of a beautiful rose take shape. Then I heard a voice in my head say, 'Don't be frightened, it's me, Thérèse.' There was a gentle breeze blowing that afternoon and all I can say is that as the breeze blew against my body it seemed to contain a deep peace and love; it was as if the breeze was made of love itself. I suddenly began to feel very emotional and I wanted to cry.

'Why have you come to me again?' I asked.

'I know you have a great devotion to God,' came the reply. 'But I want you to trust Him even more. I want you to pray to Him even more.' As these words were being spoken it was as if I was being enveloped in a fire, a fire of love. I could feel it all around me and through me and as I looked at the wall again the image of the rose was now so brilliantly intense it was hard to look at it for more than a second. I closed my eyes and the voice said, 'Stay with me, my child. I'm always with you, your prayers are always answered.'

I was trembling, trembling with ecstasy, and when I opened my eyes the image of the rose had gone from the wall, but I had the same sensation as I did when Saint Thérèse visited me previously. I felt renewed, as if I had been given a new source of beautiful strength.

I learned some time later that Saint Thérèse of Lisieux is sometimes referred to as 'The Little Flower of Jesus'; she had a great devotion to God and became a Carmelite nun at a very young age. Both her parents were very religious. Her father, Louis, had attempted to become a monk, but was refused because he knew no Latin. Her mother,

Azélie, was rejected as a nun because she was considered to have no vocation; instead, she asked God to give her many children and let them all be consecrated to God. Louis and Azélie met in 1858 and married only three months later. They had nine children, of whom only five daughters – Marie, Pauline, Leonie, Celine and Thérèse – survived to adulthood. Thérèse was their youngest child.

I have Eamon to thank for both of Thérèse's unexpected visits to me. But Eamon isn't only a conduit between the world of spirit and myself, he is also one of the most practical, helpful and loving entities I've come to know; in a strange way he almost has a human quality to him. I consider him one of my best friends. He was a source of endless support and advice as I was really worried about the consequences of changing my name and the effect it might have on my family. But he assured me that Fran would, in time, completely come round to the idea. He also confirmed to me that what the angel on the mountainside in Donegal had told me to do was absolutely correct. Eamon said that more and more would be revealed to me as I continued on my journey with the angels.

I have to say that from the moment I left the mountainside I could actually feel the old me slipping away. In some inexplicable way it truly was as if I had always been Francesca Brown. It felt to me that Penelope Gibbs was an experience that I had needed to go through, and having done so I was now ready to assume my true identity once more. I say once more because from the moment the name Francesca Brown was mentioned to me I felt that I already knew her intimately. For me, stepping into this new identity was like picking up an old glove and putting it on your hand, knowing quite well that it would fit perfectly because you had worn it before.

As time went on, not only did the name change seem the right thing to do, it seemed the natural thing to do. But of course it wasn't just me that would be affected if I went out and took on a new identity. How it would affect the people around me was a big concern.

But Eamon was right about Fran. I could see a gradual change in him; he was becoming more and more interested in the whole spiritual world and the idea that angels existed. This was helped by the fact that Angel Anne would often give me a piece of information – perhaps about a certain person we knew and a change that was about to happen in their life, or even about some direction a world event was going to take – and it would also come about. In the beginning I think this just fascinated Fran but now it was beginning to have a deeper impact on him; he was definitely developing a serious interest in the presence of angels. However, he was still very much the practical one when it came to the idea of me taking on a completely new identity in life. One of his main concerns was what effect it would have on our children.

Jason was fifteen at the time and Dwayne was thirteen. We decided that we would try and break the news of the name change slowly and Fran had the idea of first suggesting that Francesca Brown would be a name that I would be using when I was seeing or talking to people about the presence of angels. He felt that this would give the boys a chance to come to terms with the new name, without completely taking Penelope Gibbs from their lives.

To both our surprise, it worked very well and it didn't

seem to bother either of the boys at all. They both have a great sense of humour and they would come in from school and say things to me like, 'Hi Penny, I mean Francesca, no I mean Penny – don't I?' They did seem to take it all in their stride and that had the effect of relieving quite a bit of stress between Fran and I.

I was surprised one evening when Fran turned to me and said, 'You know you become a different woman when you talk about angels.'

'Do I really? In what way?' I asked him.

'Well, you take on different mannerisms,' he replied. 'Your hand gestures change; you become animated and your voice even seems to change to an extent. It's as if it's you but it's not you; it's as if there's something behind you that's expressing itself.'

The conversation surprised me a little. It seemed we were beginning to share a better understanding about the angels and their wish to work with me.

This made me very happy and once again Eamon was correct because he always told me I wasn't going to have to take this journey with the angels completely by myself.

# 6

## Joanna

Word had begun to spread around my neighbourhood and even further afield about my connection with the angels and more and more people began to arrive at my door wanting to know if I could help them establish their own connection with the angels.

I was absolutely delighted by this, as I love to use any chance I get to talk about the angels and my experiences with them, especially as a lot of new angels and spirit guides had begun making themselves known to me.

This was a very good time for me; I could see big changes beginning to happen in my personality, and certain things that used to interest me or seem important to me just didn't any more. For example, I was always a big reader of romantic fiction but now these books just didn't hold any interest for me. The same thing happened with my choice in music: I just couldn't listen to many of the singers and artists that I used to love. I could see changes beginning to happen in my personal relationships as well: people with whom I had been friends for many years began to drop away, and sometimes I would even have to get up and just leave someone's company. It was nothing to do with the people themselves, they were the same as they always were, but it just didn't feel right for me to be there any more. I would often find myself asking what I was doing in certain social situations and I would have to leave.

So there were big changes going on in my life when a little spirit guide named Joanna introduced herself to me one day. She first appeared to me in my house in Blanchardstown one afternoon. A slight, beautiful little spirit girl with golden brown curls, piercing grey eyes and a big bright smile.

I had walked into our dining room when suddenly I became aware of a sense of children playing in the room. I could actually hear their voices as they squealed with delight and had fun. Then I saw the shape of this lovely little girl become more and more real. I was taken aback with her energy, although she seemed a little wary of me. She was somehow different from anything I had experi-enced in the angel realm or the spirit world before, in a totally pure, untouched, childlike way.

I gazed at her in wonder, this mischievous, almost tomboy-like child, and after a little while I asked her, 'Who are you?' She was shy and hesitated before she answered.

'I'm Joanna and I'm going to be able to help you with your work sometimes.' I then asked where she came from.

'I live in the light,' she replied. 'I died from leukemia when I was six years old and now I'm in heaven.' I asked her how she would be able to help me.

'Well,' she replied, 'Joseph lets me look after the children who have just passed into heaven and I'll be there with you if anyone needs help after their baby has passed on.'

I was totally stunned by this statement.

'Who is Joseph?' I asked her.

'Joseph is an angel, he's funny and lovely and he takes

care of all the babies that have just passed over,' she said. Then she slightly turned away from me.

'What's wrong? You've gone all shy on me,' I gently probed.

'I don't know if I can tell you, Joseph might not allow me,' she said rather doubtfully. Another few moments passed and then she said, 'Sure, it's OK, I can tell you. Three babies have just passed and I'm very excited. I'm going to be looking after them.'

At the same time as Joanna was relating this information she was also letting me see the most beautiful sight. I suppose you would call it a nursery scene, but not like any nursery I'd ever seen before. I could see Joanna there with other childlike figures, roughly around the same age as her and all emanating a very calm, beautiful placid energy. They were all looking after these beautiful babies in rows of cots.

I was stunned and wanted to cry, it was so wonderful. Then Joanna said, 'If you look in the newspaper you will see the three babies' names that have just passed.' I went out that evening and I just instinctively knew to purchase a copy of Dublin's *Evening Herald* and there in the death columns was a notice of three infant babies who had just died.

I was overwhelmed and I didn't know what to say or think. On the one hand I was filled with remorse for these poor three babies whose lives had been cut so short, but it was as if I couldn't be sad after I had seen the vision that Joanna had revealed to me of how these infants were being cared for. I cried, but I also felt joyous and so grateful.

I cut the notice out from the paper and I still have it to

this day. I also thought of trying to get in touch with the parents of these precious infants and trying to tell them that everything was all right, but I decided against it as Joanna hadn't elaborated or suggested to me that I should do so.

Some time had passed after my first encounter with Joanna when, again in my home in Blanchardstown, she materialised and we spoke for a while. As we were speaking I became aware that she seemed distant, a little withdrawn and her energy wasn't as bright as before. I asked if everything was alright.

'I'm sad today because I miss my "Baby Born" dolly,' she said. 'I've always loved my dolly, but Mammy didn't put her in the coffin with me because she loved her too and she reminded her of me. So she put her on her dresser in her bedroom, but I miss my dolly.' I immediately felt I had to ask Joanna if she would like another Baby Born? She instantly lit up and beamed.

'Oh yes,' she replied. 'I'd really like another dolly, yes please.'

Well that was that. Her request had such a profound effect on me that I put out an SOS among my friends and family to find a second Baby Born doll for Joanna. But locating one wasn't as easy a task as it sounded, as the manufacturers were no longer making them. However, my mother is a great woman for rummaging through second-hand shops and markets and, sure enough, two days later she rang me with the news that she had found a Baby Born doll. When I got the doll home I realised that its clothes were a bit shabby, so I persuaded Fran to accompany me to Smith's toyshop in the city centre, where, despite Fran's mutterings of 'we must be losing our minds', we eventually found some clothes that fitted our new Baby Born.

With the doll now dressed in her new outfit, I entered into meditation and reached Joanna. She jumped with joy and was absolutely delighted when she saw her new dolly. I asked her if she was as nice as her last doll. She nodded.

'Just as nice and Mammy can still have the first one,' she said.

That doll has had pride of place in my meditation room for a number of years now and has become what I can only describe as a healing doll. So much so that people often comment on the doll and the energy that she radiates with remarks such as, 'The doll's eyes seem to be following me', or, as one woman put it, 'That doll is playing peek-a-boo with me, I feel there's a child behind her.'

And Joanna has proved herself to be a remarkable guide and helper whenever I have someone with me who has suffered the loss of a child. If I'm with someone and she appears I just say to her, 'Joanna do I have someone here who has lost a baby?' and if the response is in the positive I know I can go on from there and Joanna will help. Sometimes she will just be there in the background and it's enough that her loving, healing energy is present; the person will feel it.

During meditation classes that I ran for many months in my home in Blanchardstown the doll often drew people to her. One lady who had lost a young baby could not be parted from the doll over a course of eight meditation classes; she refused to let the doll out of her sight and held her closely. As she was doing this I could see Joanna materialise in spirit and comfort the woman as she caressed the doll. That woman was a different person when she left the classes. She said to me, 'All I know is that doll has given me more healing than all the bereavement classes that I've attended put together and even though I got a lot out of those classes, I know that my child was in that doll.' Joanna and Baby Born had done their healing work.

I don't know how best to really describe Joanna's personality to you. If I said that you wouldn't really want to trust her with your greatest secret because she'd only have to go and tell someone, it might begin to describe her – mischievous, sparkling and full of fun. She very definitely has that energy that a lot of children who have passed to the spirit world at a young age have. Many people refer to this energy as poltergeist activity, quite wrongly in my opinion. Joanna was full of life and loved to play while she was here on Earth and she still does; I know it's as simple as that.

Fran and I also quickly found out that she absolutely adores Noddy cartoons. How did we find this out? Well on several occasions before we went to bed we'd do the usual checks and see that the television and other electrical items were all unplugged before turning the lights off and making our way upstairs. In the morning, when we'd come down to face the day, lo and behold, the television would be on, and always showing Noddy cartoons! That's Joanna for you.

But there was one occasion when Joanna appeared to me and truly astonished me. On this occasion she had three other small children with her, two girls and a boy all aged about three years. I asked her who the children were and where they had come from.

'They've all passed into heaven and I'm looking after them,' she replied. Then she asked me a question.

'Do you know the little boy with me?' she asked.

'No, how would I?' I replied. Her answer dumbfounded me.

'Well, he's your little boy, his name is Ben,' she replied.

I was completely shocked. I had suffered a miscarriage early in my marriage and both Fran and I had agreed that if we had had a little boy then we would have called him Ben. I began to weep uncontrollably.

'Don't be sad,' said Joanna. 'By now you must know that all the children are looked after who have passed to the light and there's no need to be sad. Look at how happy he is.' And it was true, Ben did appear to be carefree and radiantly happy.

'Say bye-bye to Ben now and just let him be with us,' said Joanna. And that is exactly what I was able to do, but it was with a grace and understanding that I had received from Joanna. I will always be grateful to her for letting me have a glimpse of what my son, Ben, would have been like if he had been born into a life here on earth.

The reason Joanna first contacted me was to let me know that she would be there if I had someone who needed help after they had suffered the loss of a young child. So, of course, a great many of the times that she came through to me were in difficult and very unhappy circumstances.

I once had a visit from a woman who lived in the north Dublin suburb of Ballymun. As the woman began to speak to me she was very emotional and quickly became upset, and I knew immediately that she had suffered a great loss. Then Joanna appeared with a lovely little girl by her side, about two years old. She gently gestured towards the little girl as if to say just let her speak.

The little girl said, 'That's my mammy you have with you now.' I immediately explained to the woman that the little girl had come through to me and had said that she was her mammy. But to my surprise the woman denied this, although it was evident that she was getting more and more upset. I was perplexed because Joanna had never been wrong about any piece of information that she had any part in relaying to me and I trusted her totally. The matter was quickly cleared up, however, when the woman spoke up.

'No, I'm not the girl's natural mammy but I reared her; she's my sister's child.' As she made this statement something occurred that quite often happens to me when I'm in contact with someone who has passed to the world of spirit in difficult or even violent circumstances. I begin to feel and experience the actual physical symptoms of their passing.

And so it was with this little girl, who unfortunately had drowned in a swimming pool in Majorca in Spain. I won't go into what those symptoms were as it would serve no useful purpose and if this phenomenon upsets anyone I would point out that the experience passes very quickly once I fully establish contact with the person who has passed. I was able to do this very quickly with this little girl, with Joanna's help.

But the whole story was a very tragic one. The woman explained to me that her sister, the little girl's mother, was a drug addict in Dublin and she died from a drug overdose some years ago. So she had taken over the responsibility of raising her niece as her own, and she loved her as if she was her own daughter. But then tragedy followed tragedy and when on holiday in Spain the little girl suffered a horrible death by drowning in a swimming pool. There is only one reason that I am relating this story now and that is to demonstrate the amazing power that Joanna has to heal. As that poor woman in front of me cried and groped for the words to try and explain the horror of what had happened to both her sister and her little niece, Joanna appeared and with her were two other people.

One was a young woman who was very thin and had deep blue eyes and the other was an elderly lady who seemed very frail in body but gave the impression of being made of sterner stuff. Joanna spoke: 'This is the little girl's mammy and her grandmother. You must let the woman know that everything is as it is in the world of light and everything is all right; there's no need to be sad or to be worried.'

As I looked on I could see the little girl, her mother and her grandmother together and there was a real sense of peace about them, a sense of oneness, of unity. Then the little girl spoke, still referring to her aunt as her mother: 'My mammy has a photo of me in her pocket. Tell her to take it out and look at it.' I told the lady to do as she had said. The photo was taken in a playground and the little girl looked blissfully happy, playing on a swing and laughing.

'Tell her I'm as happy today as I was then,' she said. I relayed this information to the woman and she buried her head in her hands and sobbed and sobbed. 'But you really must listen to what your niece has told you today,' I gently told her. With that, she got up and we hugged and I knew that although there might be hard times ahead for that woman, she had received a realisation of healing through Joanna.

But I also had some very funny and unusual moments with Joanna. I remember well the day a lady with a little deaf girl came to visit me in Blanchardstown. The little girl was immediately drawn to playing with Joanna's Baby Born dolly. So taken was she with the doll that she didn't put it down for the entire time her mother was with me – well over an hour. Then, when it was time to leave, the little girl reluctantly put the doll back down on the settee where she had found her. But as the pair were leaving and making their way out the door, Joanna suddenly appeared and said to me, 'Tell that girl's mother that her daughter has magic in her feet.' So I stopped the woman and told her what Joanna had just said.

'Does your daughter dance? Is she a good dancer?' I enquired, slightly mystified by Joanna's remark.

'No, she's not a dancer. I don't understand what that means,' replied her mother.

Some weeks went by, until one day I had a knock on my door and it was the lady and her little daughter. I asked them in and enquired how everything was.

'Well, I felt I just had to come and tell you this little story,' replied her mother. 'Two days after I left you my daughter began to feel a soreness in her feet and I took her to our local doctor. He didn't know quite what was wrong with her so he sent her to Temple Street Children's Hospital to have some X-rays done. When he returned with the X-rays he simply said, "Your daughter has magic feet, she had an extra little bone in each foot. It's not serious and it won't cause her any great problems."' Well, we both laughed and laughed.

But that wasn't the only fun we've had with Joanna. When we first got her new Baby Born doll my two young sons, Jason and Dwayne, didn't quite know what to make of the situation. Perhaps they even felt that they were being left out of the picture somewhat with all this attention being paid to a doll that they had never seen before. So they decided they would have a little bit of fun with Baby Born. One night, when Fran and I came back from the pictures, Fran looked around and couldn't see the doll anywhere.

'Where's Joanna's doll gone? Did someone move her?' he asked. We searched the house over and over but there was still no sign of the doll and I began to think that someone must have taken her from the house. Then my two sons began to giggle a little and say things like, 'Oh, I'm sure she's around here somewhere, *up* there or *down* here, or somewhere.' So I looked up at the chandelier that we had in our dining room and there, sitting right on top of it, was Joanna's dolly. Of course, my two boys knew absolutely *nothing* about how she might have got up there! But at that moment I glimpsed a view of Joanna and she was holding her sides and roaring with laughter.

# 7

# The Power of the Spirits

One aspect of my work with the angel realm and the spirit world that never fails to amaze and inform me is the power of children who have passed over into the light.

Of course, the main reason for this is my relationship with Joanna and the sheer joy and indeed contentment I've seen her bring to people's lives after they have unfortunately lost a child. But the energy that some children have after they have passed over is a true wonder.

A lot of people refer to this as poltergeist activity but it's not a term that I have much time for. To me, it's all very simple: when they are alive, children can be playful, bored, energetic, happy, sad, loving, rude or even hateful. Well, things don't appear to change that much when some of them enter into the world of spirit.

I can recall very well the first time I really witnessed just how powerful the energy of a child who has passed on can be. A very good neighbour of mine, Catherine, called into me one afternoon for a cup of tea and a chat. She had already mentioned to me on a couple of occasions that a couple she knew very well from Northern Ireland had lost their little baby boy at only two weeks old. These unfortunate parents had asked Catherine if there was any possibility that I might be able to reach the spirit of their little boy. I have to admit that when I was first asked I simply didn't know if it was possible or not. I had never been asked to try and contact the spirit of someone so young before. So I said that I would try.

When I went to the angels and asked for their help the spirit of an old lady appeared and told me she was an aunt of the infant who had passed to the light. When I first relayed this information back to the little boy's parents they said they couldn't recall any aunt of the description that I gave them. However, apparently when they mentioned the aunt to some other members of their family it transpired that there was indeed an aunt who had died a long time ago. It also turned out that this aunt was actually buried very close to where the young boy was, in an old grave-yard near the couple's home in Northern Ireland.

At this point I had been channelling poems from the angels for some months and Catherine asked me if I would channel a poem for them. This I readily agreed to do and when I got the poem I had a very strong feeling that this little infant's energy was very much contained in it.

I had got into the habit of framing some of my poems from the angels, usually the ones that I particularly liked myself. I would hang them around my meditation room, where I noticed that many people were drawn to them and enjoyed reading them. When I received the poem for the little boy's parents I felt it was special, so I decided that I would have it framed for the couple. I went ahead and took the poem in to be framed, and when Catherine called in again I told her what I had done. When I got the poem back from the framing shop I phoned Catherine and told her it was ready but to my surprise she said that now she didn't want it. I really don't know why she had changed her mind but perhaps she felt the infant's parents needed more time to come to terms with their loss. So I decided I would just hang the poem on the wall in my meditation room. Many of the poems I channel from the angels have a feeling and presence about them that is difficult to explain in words and this poem had a huge presence about it. I felt the little boy's energy was very much in this poem.

The poem hung on my wall for nearly a year, until one day Catherine came to visit me and said, 'You remember the poem that I asked you to channel from the angels for the couple from Northern Ireland who had just lost their little boy?' I said I remembered it well.

'Well, the parents are coming down to Dublin soon and I'd really like to take the poem now, if you still have it?' I told her the poem was still hanging on my wall and I'd be delighted for the couple to have it.

It was a Saturday when the couple from Northern Ireland arrived at my house to collect their poem. It's strange, but there was a feeling of great expectation in the air that day, rather like the feeling you might get about an early spring day: very energetic. There were several other people present when the couple arrived, including Fran, Catherine and Janet – another neighbour of mine. I welcomed them both and we hugged each other. Time, as they say, is a great healer, but I could feel from this couple's energy that they had been through a very hard time emotionally.

We made a cup of tea and chatted for a little while and then I said, 'Would you like to see where I've had your poem hanging?' The couple nodded and smiled, so I led everyone into my meditation room. What happened next made everyone jump with sheer fright and duck for cover! A streak of what I can only describe as red-orange lightning flashed across the room and hit the poem full blast in the face. It jumped from its spot on the wall and came crashing to the ground where it lay, its laminated coating smouldering from where it had taken the full force of the blast. There was a smell of something like gunpowder in the room and a small pall of smoke lingered over where the poem lay on the ground. When the streak of fiery energy first hit the poem everyone had jumped and ducked but now there was an eerie silence in the room; we were all just stunned and lost for words. Fran was the first to speak.

'What in the name of God was that?' he said (in fact what he said was far more colourful but I won't repeat it here!). Then everyone began to speak at once. It was as if Fran had taken the cork out of the bottle and now we all needed to voice something about what we had just witnessed because it was so extraordinary. Fran bent down to pick the poem up but he quickly dropped it again.

'Wow!' he exclaimed. It seemed the poem had retained some of the energy of the blast and was still full of static electricity.

So there we sat, in my meditation room, all looking at the poem on the ground. It now made rather a sorry sight, as a brownish-black scorch mark could clearly be seen on its covering where it had been struck by the blast. Nobody in that room really knew what had happened that afternoon. However, everyone present was left with the very strong impression that the energy of that little infant was somehow very much involved. To me personally it was almost as if he was saying, 'I'm here; don't forget about me, I'm here.'

Although the spirit of that little boy had never communicated directly with me from the spirit world, from the first instance when I had contact with his aunt I was very much aware of his energy. On that afternoon in Blanchardstown he showed in no uncertain terms that he was there – boy did he show it! His parents left my home different people. The little boy's mother held her son's poem firmly in her hands; they seemed so much closer together.

This was the first time I had dramatically witnessed the power that children who have passed to the spirit world possess, but it wasn't by any means the last time.

One day, a lady came to visit me. She was at her wits' end with worry. She lived close to me in an area called Mulhuddart in west Dublin and some very strange activity taking place in her home had her and her family extremely frightened. She explained to me that doors would bang by themselves, lights would go on and off by themselves and furniture could be seen moving across the floor by itself. Seeing that the woman genuinely needed help, I agreed I would come to her home the following day and see if I could figure out what was going on.

When I entered her home, I immediately knew that it was a child that was causing the mysterious happenings. I sensed the child before I actually saw anyone. It wasn't in any way a bad or frightening sensation, at least not for me. Fran had come along with me and the woman had invited us into her front room. It wasn't long after Christmas and the Christmas tree was still up and several toys lay scattered around on the floor.

Then something happened that startled us all: a child's

remote control car that was on the floor started moving around the room by itself! The woman's reaction to this was to freeze in terror while Fran and I just looked on in amazement as the car shot around on the floor all by itself. The woman then took her feet up off the ground and held herself by her knees – just as you might see someone do if a mouse came into a room and they were very afraid of mice.

'There isn't even a battery in it,' she squealed, looking at the car with terror in her eyes. The car came to a stop and Fran went over and picked it up, and sure enough there was no battery in it. But as he picked up the car I heard a little girl's voice utter the words, 'My toys.' There was an indignant tone to the words, as a child would utter when someone else, especially another child, was trying to play with their toys. The woman then explained that the car had been a Christmas present for her young son. But he hadn't been able to play with it because it wouldn't work when the battery was put into it and then, as we'd all witnessed, it would fly around the room with no battery in it, terrifying everyone. The family's Christmas had been ruined and the situation had become so extreme that the woman and her husband had actually moved their children out of the house and had them staying with their grandparents. They had also called in a local priest to bless the house but the strange happenings continued.

I really felt for the woman and her family; they were very scared and becoming quite desperate. I asked her to explain the whole story to me: when the activity had begun and exactly what was happening in the house and where. She explained that they bought the house from another couple and that they hadn't been in the house very long when the activity had begun. But in the beginning it was only little things, like the tap would be found running after it was turned off, and for a long time they thought they were imagining things.

Gradually, however, the activity became more and more frightening to the family: doors would slam for no reason; lights would flicker and come on and off by themselves; a window had burst open by itself in one of the children's rooms; and – something that the woman herself found to be the most frightening of phenomena – the temperature in some of the rooms would drop to be very cold in an instant.

I asked her if there was any place in the house where the activity was worse than elsewhere. She nodded and said in her eldest daughter's bedroom. I asked her to show me the room and she agreed, although I could see that going up to the room was the last thing she wanted to do at that moment. As we made our way up the stairs, the woman leading Fran and I, there was a colossal bang.

'Jesus Christ!' exclaimed the woman, turning back and actually trying to squeeze her way past us – nearly knocking us over in the process. 'That's it, I'm not going in there,' she said, pointing at a bedroom door. 'I know it's just the door of the wardrobe banging, but it's banging by itself.'

'It's OK, I'll go in,' I soothed her. I left Fran and the woman outside on the landing and I opened the door to her daughter's room. It was quite a large bedroom with a bed, wardrobe and dresser. The moment I was fully inside the room I knew there was a spirit present. Call it a sixth sense, but when a spirit enters or is already present in a room I sense it, just like someone senses another human being when they enter a room.

Standing on the far side of the bed was a little girl, aged perhaps six or seven, and she seemed to be just looking at the bed. When I looked at her I knew that the spirit of this little girl, who was causing all this trouble, meant nobody any real harm.

'What is your name?' I gently asked her. It was as if she was about to answer me but she couldn't. Instead, she gave me a slightly quizzical look as if she was slightly confused and with that she disappeared. I was left alone in the room but the little girl's energy had now become clearer to me. I felt a lot of frustration around her, a sense of her being annoyed with someone and that she was lonely, very lonely. I wanted to reach out and to comfort her, to hug her. I wished she would reappear, but she didn't.

I went out of the bedroom and joined Fran and the woman on the landing and we all went back down to the front room. I explained to her that there was the spirit of a little girl in her house and I felt that she was somehow trapped but she didn't mean anyone any harm. She had a lot of energy about her and that was what was causing all the strange phenomena throughout the house. I asked her if she had any candles in the house, as burning a candle is a wonderful way of gently dispelling any atmosphere from a particular place. So we lit a candle and put it on a table in the centre of the room. I sat down, became quiet and asked the angels to come to the aid of the spirit of this little girl, who was clearly so unhappy for some reason. Quite quickly I could feel a sense of release; it wasn't so much a sense of her spirit leaving but more a sense of a returning, a returning home, a sense of something being settled. I had the feeling that whatever this little girl's problems were, with the help of the angels they had now been clarified for her. I don't know if that makes much sense but that is what I felt that day in that room.

I told the woman who owned the house that I didn't think she would have any further problems, but if she did to contact me. I never heard from her again. I don't know if that little girl actually lived in that house, or close by, at some stage of her life on earth, but there is no doubt that spirits can and do become very attached to certain places and buildings here on earth. I remember one instance when this was brought home to me in a very dramatic way, although it didn't involve the spirit of a child.

One nice spring day, Fran and I, along with two of our friends – Kathy and Keith, decided we would go for a drive in the countryside and so we headed for the Hill of Slane in County Meath. It was a wonderful day for walking and the four of us set off with no particular destination in mind – we were just enjoying the afternoon. But the afternoon was about to be rudely disrupted for me.

We were walking through the ruins of an old abbey when we came to a clearing and sat down on a fence to take a little rest. Kathy and I had known each other for years and she was also interested in the spiritual world of the angels. She was delighted for me and always encouraged me with my work. As we sat chatting she made a comment about the Hill of Slane being a very ancient and spiritual place.

'Why don't you try and see if you can contact any spirits here?' she said in a casual way. And without really thinking

I replied, 'OK, is there anyone here?' With that, I got a really hard slap across my face and a stern voice said, 'The Reverend Philip Dwyer.' I was very shocked. I hadn't seen anyone; I just got this blow to my face and heard the voice. The others all heard the slap but not the voice and they were astonished.

'What the hell was that?' asked Kathy.

'I don't know,' I replied. 'I've just had a really hard slap across the face and a voice said "The Reverend Philip Dwyer" to me.'

'Oh my God, don't say that,' said Kathy fearfully.

'Oh, don't worry, it's probably just some spirit letting us know that he's around the place,' I replied, but I must admit I didn't really want to stay around for any longer than I had to.

So we all began to move off and walk again, but I could still very much feel the presence of whoever or whatever had given me such a rude awakening a few moments earlier. As we walked we came upon the ruins of a small old grave-yard. It was a very picturesque place so we entered and began to walk around it, looking at the old graves. Suddenly Kathy let out a squeal.

'Oh Jesus, look at that, I don't believe it.' She was standing over an old grave with her hand over her mouth and I could see that she was really shocked. I went over to her and asked what the matter was. She took a step backwards and just pointed at the grave. I turned and looked at it and there on the headstone were the words 'The Reverend Philip Dwyer'. I must admit the hairs did stand up on the back of my neck when I saw the name and the feeling or presence that I had felt when I got the slap across the face was now very strong indeed. One thing was obvious: this place was still very much the Reverend Dwyer's place and I was pretty sure he wasn't pleased with us intruding!

Then Fran pointed out that there were other gravestones with the surname Dwyer on them as well. It was clear that the Reverend had many of his family or ancestors buried around him. We decided it was best that we leave so we quietly made our way out of the graveyard. It wasn't until we had walked about 300 metres away that I felt the presence of the Reverend Dwyer had left me; it was as if I knew we had just left his domain.

That story dramatically demonstrates the fact that spirits, and not just the spirits of children, can become very attached to places and to people that are still here on earth. Some of those spirits can express themselves very powerfully, sometimes causing all kinds of fear and trepidation for anyone who happens to encounter them and doesn't understand what exactly is happening or why.

But it's not only the spirits of people who are in some way trapped or unhappy that can inhabit certain places here on earth. I've also come across many very happy and indeed jolly spirits who just seem to enjoy revisiting certain places that were special to them while they were alive.

# 8

## The Child Within All of Us

The world of the angels, being a reflection of God's world, is a very wondrous world indeed. The realisations that can occur within that world never cease to stun me, amaze me and make me give eternal thanks that I have the angels to travel with me along life's journey and, of course, so do you. The sheer sense of fun and childlike enjoyment that is available to each and every one of us through making a connection with the angels is truly wondrous; it is a real gift from God.

Remember that every child is born with the feeling of sheer love for God within itself. That is why a small baby will lie gurgling with happiness as it stares straight ahead, just blissful in the feeling or sensation of joy that lies within itself, within its small body. It does this without any prompting from its parents or anybody else. One look at the sheer smile of joy on a baby's face is enough to convince anyone that it is experiencing total bliss as the natural feeling of itself. Unfortunately that feeling of natural bliss doesn't last for long, as the world with all its problems and unhappiness begins to impose itself on the child; it's really quite a tragedy.

We all contribute to gradually drawing the child out from its own natural state of joyful being and into our world.

We don't mean to cause the child any harm of course, far from it, nearly all of us only wish the very best for all our children. But that is what happens. The child slowly begins to lose the feeling of the natural joy within, as it is encouraged to swap the natural feeling of itself for that of a rattle, or a doll, or for some brightly coloured soft toys. Gradually the child starts to rely on these things that are outside of itself for its happiness. It forgets its true self, as it comes to rely on the world outside more and more. This becomes very clear when the external things the child is now seeking its joy from, like the rattle or the doll, are removed. When this happens, the child has less of the natural joy of itself to fall back on and it can quickly become very upset and demanding.

At first, when the small child was just lying there complete in the joy of itself, everything was complete and there was nothing to want, assuming that it was being fed and clothed, but now it begins to need more and more things; it is rapidly heading for unhappiness.

Every parent knows just how emotionally demanding and angry a small child can get as it begins to frown and scowl and fly into tantrums. This is due to the increasing unhappiness within the child as it becomes more and more reliant on the external world around itself and forgets its true self.

I'm not suggesting that children should be denied their toys and their dolls, far from it, but at the same time I think it would be wonderful if we could keep our children in touch with that natural joy that lies within each and every child. This is exactly what making a connection with angels can do. It can bring us back to that natural state of joyfulness that lies within each and every one of us – we've just forgotten that it's there, as our world of dolls and rattles turns into a world of mortgages and bank overdrafts.

That connection is needed more and more in our daily lives today. It seems to me that men, women and children are being dragged head first into a world of consumerism and materialism, and it's a sterile place full of meaningless gadgets and super-clever computerised devices. But where has the natural joy that lies within us all gone? How can we begin to return to the simple joy of just being? Making a connection with the angel realm can do that for us, if we can just muster enough faith and belief to allow it to be manifest in our lives.

Many, many times I have asked the angels, why me? Why have I been given this wondrous gift to communicate with them so freely and easily? They have told me that it is my destiny, that I have travelled many, many lifetimes and that I have finally come home to be with them and with God. All I can say when I hear this from them is that I am totally humbled. I don't really know what to say. I must also admit that I don't fully understand it all, but I also know as I speak these words that I don't fully need to understand it all. I sometimes wonder who it is that wants to understand it all – to understand everything. I believe it is mostly my mind and my mind can never fully understand God – I am sure of that. So I just relax with it, with the angels.

The angels' world is a totally wondrous place, full of fun, surprises and a childlike innocence. This fact is being constantly brought home to me in a variety of different ways.

I must admit it did come as a surprise to me when I first became aware that the angels love fairy tales, they simply love them! What surprised me even more was when they explained to me the reasons why they love them. They love them because they are true! Does that sound ridiculous? Perhaps it does. I was also surprised the first time the spirit guide Joanna told me the reason she loved fairy tales – because they are true! I feel what the angels and Joanna were really trying to say is that they love fairy tales because they know that they are based on the truth. You could say that the people who wrote the fairy tales were doing so from a sense of truth deep within their subconscious when they wrote all those lovely tales long ago.

Take *The Wizard of Oz*, one of Joanna's and my own favourite fairy tales. First written by a man called L. Frank Baum well over 100 years ago, it tells the tale of a young girl, Dorothy, who lives on a farm in Kansas but who dreams of being in a better place 'somewhere over the rainbow'. After being struck by a tornado, she dreams that she is transported to the magical land of Oz, where she meets the Good Witch of the North, Glinda, who advises her to follow the Yellow Brick Road to the Emerald City, where the Wizard of Oz will show her how to return to Kansas.

Along the way, Dorothy meets the Tin Man, who has no heart, the Scarecrow, who has no brain and the Lion, who has no courage. In the fairy tale, all three of these characters eventually discover that they all possess qualities that they thought they did not have. Dorothy is resigned to spending the rest of her life in the land of Oz until Glinda appears and tells her that she has always had the power to return home. Glinda explains that she did not tell Dorothy at first because she needed to find that out for herself.

'The next time I go looking for my heart's desire, I won't look any further than my own backyard; if it's not there, then I never really lost it to begin with,' exclaims Dorothy on discovering the truth.

I believe the message contained within the tale – that the ability to discover our true selves lies within us – is what makes *The Wizard of Oz* such an appealing fairy tale. It contains that kernel of truth that all good fairy tales have. That's what makes fairy tales so appealing to us – they are based on the truth of all of us. It's also the reason why Joanna is so fond of them.

According to the angels, words can never really explain God; they just can't. But remarkably the truth behind simple fairy tales can be very effective in getting closer to the truth than any words can. Now I know that fairy tales are conveyed in words, but it's not the words that are really important, it's the message contained within them. The very same is true for legends such as King Arthur and the Knights of the Round Table; there is something contained within these stories that penetrates very deeply down into our subconscious. That is why we are left with such a sense of wonder and joy when we read one of these classic fairy tales or legends. The reason that they have stood the test of time is not because they are so well written, nor is it because they invoke such a response in our imaginations. No, it is because they contain that grain of truth that is indestructible.

Angels love to deal in symbols, and this is for the very

same reason that fairy tales are packed with symbols: they are a way of getting closer to the truth – of getting closer to the truth of God.

Fairy tales symbolise things that are fundamental to us as human beings: beauty; love; compassion; hope; and immortality. If we look closely at fairy tales we will see that they have no past, no present and no future. They are, in reality, the *spirit* engaging in storytelling, which because it comes from the spirit, has truth in it. The human *mind* isn't interested in establishing whether there is any truth in fairy tales, all the mind is interested in is if they are true or false and of course, while the *mind* may like to read fairy tales, it will never accept that there may be truth contained within them.

One of my favourite fairy tales is *Peter Pan*. The story represents the light that radiates out for all to see – the light that keeps us young and joyful. This light teaches us how to journey between our worlds, a world of love and beauty, and a world that contains everything that you wish for in your life. Peter Pan is a child of light, a child of beauty and joy. In his world he travels to many places to find the wisdom and knowledge that he needs to find the secret of eternal youth. He flies through the universe at night, travelling through the many galaxies of life and knowing that his life is a never-ending journey where his imagination soars, taking him into an area of life where the well of abundance awaits him.

He does not fear for he knows that in his journey every-thing is divinely guided, giving him everything he needs at that moment. Peter Pan has many companions as he travels. He teaches us that the beauty of life is the inner child that lives within all of us. That inner child is young and vibrant and knows the secret of eternal youth.

If Peter Pan appears while you are meditating, let your imagination soar taking you back once again to when you believed in the world of magic. That magic helped you create that wonderful world of joy, love, peace, prosperity and abundance, showing you that your imagination is a place where all things are made possible. And always remember, as you are reading the fairy tale of *Peter Pan*, you are reading the truth of an aspect of yourself. This is why the angels are so anxious for everyone to read and to enjoy *Peter Pan*.

I've had many fairy tales brought to my consciousness by the angels, each symbolically showing me different things. I believe some classic novels also contain the same basic element of truth within them; I will share some more of them with you.

*Huckleberry Finn* is a good example. Huck saw his world as nothing, as being poor. But in the midst of all that, his inner child pushes him beyond the boundaries of his life to discover that life is a never ending adventure. He does not care for material things but for the simple things that give him pleasure.

Huck finds gold in a cave and hands it in to the authorities. He is rewarded for his honesty and is given a shilling, which is everything to him. He knows that the joys of life are inward and by going in he seeks the answers to his life adventures. He paddles his canoe through the waters of life, knowing that everything he wants is there.

The message is contained in the tale, not really in the words; there is an energy beyond the words, isn't there?

You can sense it; it's very gentle, yet at the same time it's very powerful – now at this time in your life, trust your abilities, your hopes and dreams. Just like Huckleberry Finn, paddle your own canoe through the rivers of life knowing as you do that everything you need will be met.

Fairy tales can bring us closer to the realisation that the spiritual world is really real. Whatever we perceive through our physical senses is only partially real and when you begin to realise that the spiritual world is in fact the real world you will see things completely differently. A walk in the countryside will become more real; the sunset will become more real; flowers, trees, animals – they will all become more real. You will begin to understand that behind every physical form there lies a magic that the human mind cannot begin to really understand – the same magic that is contained within fairy tales; it's totally remarkable.

It's also remarkable to think that many of these fairy tales or myths would have been handed down by word of mouth for a long, long time before they were ever written down and recorded to become the tales that we know and love today.

Another fairy tale that the angels brought to me in meditation is the story of Aladdin and his magic lamp. This tale represents the flow of life within us – that spark of divinity that reaches out every day, offering us that well of abundance that lives within us. Aladdin's cave symbolically reaches out to show us that by journeying inward and listening to that stillness within the way will be guided for us. Aladdin's cave also helps us to learn to trust that the light that lives within will always answer when we call.

Aladdin's cave was to become a very important exercise

for me. It was here in the cave that the angels showed me those feelings of peace, joy, love and abundance that I needed in order for my manifestations to come about in the physical plane. Each morning before I got out of bed I journeyed into Aladdin's cave to meet the light of the universe that comes each day to assist me and grant me my wishes. My wishes were not for material things, because these no longer concerned me; what I needed in my life was a life-force, an energy that was bright, radiant, joyful, peaceful, motivated, ambitious, felt worthy of everything, and was confident, strong and sure of where I was going and what I had to do when I got there.

So I practised each day, asking for my life to be filled with joy, peace, love and laughter and the more I asked the more the universe answered, granting me everything that I had asked for. For this was my first step in mani-festation, taking me into an area of my life where each day was filled with beautiful thoughts and beautiful affirma-tions that have helped me get to where I am today. That is the glorious truth behind the story of Aladdin and his magic lamp.

The story or myth of the search for the Holy Grail also comes to mind, and again the message that is contained within the words is what's really important. That message is, of course, that God is found within ourselves, not up in the sky, or in special people or special places, but simply within.

Long ago, the men and women who searched for the Holy Grail, their symbol of the Kingdom of God, spent a lifetime searching only to find that it was a mistake to seek outside themselves. As they returned from their exhaustive search they were completely beaten and totally discouraged by the foolishness of their mission; they had failed utterly and they knew it. But in their state of dejection there must have been a sense of giving up, a great sense of letting go and when they did this perhaps they realised that the 'golden chalice' had been close by all along. Oh, the joy when we come to truly realise that the Kingdom of heaven is right there within us, just waiting to be realised.

But while it may be fine for me to say that the Kingdom of God is already in us and if we can only make a connection with angels then it will be revealed to us, what can we practically do to bring this about? How can we make it real within our experience? It's like telling a person with a blindfold over their eyes about all there is to see: while it may be the true to say that there is much to see, it's of no use to the person blindfolded until they can discover a way of getting rid of the blindfold. So it is with us; we must develop a consciousness that is still – still enough so that the angels can reach us and play a real part in our journey here on earth.

Remember, that is all the angels want to do; they stand ready and waiting for us to make that call and are overjoyed when we do call for their assistance. Overjoyed to be able to come to our aid, because that is their mission, to provide a divine link between God and us; they are indeed God's messengers.

Try to remember that it is within us that the connection with the angels must first be made. We have to lay out the groundwork; we have to see to it that our consciousness is still and receptive to the angels' impulse. It's not the other way around – the angels don't have to seek us out and make their presence felt – that is not the way it works at all. If you are truly earnest in your wish to create a connection with angels and if you have done all you can to establish a consciousness that is still and receptive so the angels can more easily enter it, then you will be given a sign.

The angels simply love to deal in signs and symbols and I've come across a great many different signs that have been given to people who truly wished to connect with the angels. Signs can vary: from feathers appearing out of nowhere – sometimes the most beautiful coloured feathers will appear; a beautiful fragrance may fill up your room, again from nowhere – a wonderful scent of lilac used to fill my room out of the blue; you may have a sensation that someone has just touched you – sometimes it feels like a very gentle stroke on your cheek; or people often see wonderful colours appear in front of them. There are as many signs as there are angels in the angel realm just waiting to make contact with us.

# 9

# The Key to an Abundant Life

I have mentioned before that the angels teach us that God already dwells within us. God's world is immaculate and whole; it is already complete and it is already within us. I can't tell you how important it is to grasp this simple fact – we are made from God.

I know it's easy to listen to these words and think to ourselves, 'Yes, that's fine, God is already within us' and then go on about our daily business. That's not enough – it's not nearly enough! Take, for example, the whole area of our physical health, something that is of the utmost importance to most of us. Every bookshop that you wander into these days is packed to the ceiling with different books telling us how bring about better health, through prayer, meditation, visualisation, different diets, crystals and so on. There seems to be no end to what we can do to achieve better health.

The angels have taught me that we really shouldn't be praying to God for better health for ourselves or for our families. That may come as a surprise to many of you. What we should be doing is realising the fact that God, and as a result good health, is already within us – all we have to do is realise this simple truth.

If you actually stop and think about what the angels are

trying to convey to us, you will see that it is quite different to what a lot of other people are saying today. What they are telling us to do is to simply take ourselves out of the story, and if we can do that, what are we left with? We are left with God.

If we look around at the moment, we are in throes of a recession. It seems to be everywhere, the newspapers are full of it, you can't turn on the television or the radio without being reminded just how bad things are and how much worse they are going to get. However, as we all struggle to get through what are undoubtedly hard times, and most people seem to be suffering from some sort of lack or limitation, you may notice that some people are still experiencing abundance in their lives. How can that be? Perhaps it is just luck and they've managed to avoid the worst of the recession, or maybe there is another reason. The angels have explained to me that the economic climate cannot *make* you and these tough times cannot *break* you. You, yourself, hold the answer to these apparently tough times. You hold the answer in so much as you realise that God is the substance to all form and by form I mean everything in this world – people, employment, companies, governments. So, if God is the substance to all form can you have limited form? No, of course you can't. But can you have increased form? Again, no you can't – how can you increase God? Do you see what the angels are trying to say? God is already everything, he is infinite and he is within us, we just have to realise that fact. So if you are affected by these recessionary times, like so many of us are, don't pray to God to give you anything, just pray that you realise what God already is – abundance. It's a beautifully simple message and it's the truth.

Many people have asked me if it is wrong to ask the angels for material things such as money, a better job, a bigger house, or a new car. Well, no it's not wrong to ask, because once again the angels bring us back to the true nature of God and, as a result, the true nature of ourselves. Since God is infinite, there exists nothing but God. When you really begin to perceive the infinity of God and realise that he is already there within, you can then begin to claim the infinite abundance that the angels say is already there waiting for you. Isn't that truly remarkable? It's all there within, just waiting to be released by us acknowledging the fact that it lies within, not up in the sky or anywhere else, but within this body reading these words here and now.

When you make a request of the angels for some material thing the conscious mind can be a big problem. It can get in the way; it thinks it's the boss and it can throw up many thoughts and emotions such as fear, doubt and unworthiness. The mind just can't understand that God's work is already done within us. The angels know that when we are making some material request it isn't easy for us to drop completely from our minds the doubts and concerns about finding money, or how we are going to afford to send our children to college, or buy a new car, or whatever. But drop it we must, because as we come to realise that the Kingdom of God dwells within us, we also realise that as we begin to receive more money, or the new car, these are simply outward signs of the inner good, the inner abundance that is within all of us.

The angels often like to deal in symbols and they often give me symbols that deal with many different aspects of life. However, they have made it clear to me, and I think this is so amazing, that when we make a material request for something – money, a holiday, or anything else – when that wish actually materialises in the physical realm, it is but a symbol, it is a symbol of God's infinite abundance and the supply that already lies within each and every one of us. If we don't know about God's supply and abundance in our daily lives we're not going to know about it in our purses or our bank accounts. The first thing we must consciously do is recognise God's abundance and then the symbols will follow.

When I look at it with the help of the angels it seems to me that many people tend to say things like, 'If it's God's will it will happen,' or 'With the help of God we'll get this or that,' but that's missing the point entirely. Can you begin to see that? It is only in proportion to your realisation that God *already* dwells within us that God's infinite goodness is manifested here on earth.

The angels have spoken to me about the current world recession. They are always telling me just how important it is for each and every one of us to *give*. I know that can sound a very hard thing to do, especially if you're suffering financially, but you may not necessarily even have to give anything physical, it could be that you *give up* something. Something like your fears or jealously – that is what the real spirit of giving means. I know that, as I grew to know the angels more and more, I became aware that a sense of 'spiritual pride' might begin to influence my work with them. I asked Angel Anne, and I still do, to make sure that I had the ability to give up any sense that I am somehow a special or chosen person because I have a close relationship with the angels. I'm glad to say that she constantly grounds me and keeps my feet on the ground and sometimes she doesn't mince her words with me if she feels I need it!

The whole concept of giving is based on the fact that as you give something away to someone else, it may be some money or even some clothes or food, you are giving something of your *self* away, you are actually reducing your self and creating a flow. When this happens, the nature of God, which is infinity, replenishes that which you have given away one hundred fold and it manifests in the circumstances around you.

Here is a very positive affirmation for finding a job that the angels once delivered to me. In these tough times I feel it is more relevant than ever before:

I release this situation into God's hands, knowing that the will of God already established inside of me will produce the perfect results for me, opening up that pathway for my life to be fulfilled, knowing that the perfect job now comes my way so I may prosper in everything I do.

I release. I let go. I let God.

The perfect results now manifest for me in my life today, opening up that pathway to allow only the good to enter. Leading the way so God's will may produce the perfect results, the perfect job, allowing God to work for me in the highest order, that which I already am.

I release. I let go. I let God.

Be still and know that God works in a divine order

so that the windows of light may shine upon me, opening up that doorway that will reveal my perfect job and know that God's will is my will, allowing the perfect situation to manifest in my life today.

I release. I let go. I let God.

The perfect situation now manifests in my life today, knowing as a child of God that I am worthy of everything he now gives to me today.

I release. I let go. I let God.

Here is another affirmation given to me by the angels, which has a lot of relevance today as it deals with abundance and prosperity:

The divine light of God flows within me, creating a life of total abundance, health and happiness in my life every day.

My world is full of everything I need; it is created by the source of light that lives within me.

My life is an abundant flow of living; it is rich in the substance of God freely allowing the universal light to manifest God's rich goodness in my life today and every day. This is God's will.

When I let go and know that God is the source of my supply then I will see that the one light that is rich in wealth, health, happiness and prosperity creates my life.

Then I will know that the riches of his light are mine today.

If we do decide we need to give something up it may help

if we begin with looking inward and finding the cause and effect of what we do. We may discover why we hold onto old resentments, past pain and trauma. We learn to discover that when things surface from our past that can lead to pain and resentment we need to look at those areas of our life, learn to come to an understanding of why those particular areas of our lives are still there, align them, forgive them and let them go, so that we can allow for new growth, new happiness and joy to return into all areas of our lives.

With the angels' help we can begin to learn to look at ourselves and to see the beauty and perfection within us. We learn to understand things in a more positive way, learning to let go of all old thought patterns; so it may take us into an area where our thoughts become powerful, an area where we can create the life we want.

The angels always talk about the importance of trust and faith in their work with us. They really want to help you to create the most powerful positive thought system within yourself, which in turn will help you to create the life that you richly deserve, one that is forever flowing. To achieve it, you must believe it — you must realise it.

The angels tell us to rid all negativity from our bodies – negative thoughts, negative toxins, all gossip, and critical judgement of others. Let go of all anger, all failure, and the resentment of not being good enough or worthy enough. The angels say that it is impossible for anyone to fail because we are already made of God, and once we realise this we will always manifest God's glory here on earth; even what appears to be failure can be turned around into something positive if we look at it correctly.

Look on your whole life as a blessing; bless everything

that comes your way no matter what it is, and remember that God already lies within, it's so important. Be joyful in everything you do, fill your whole being with joy, love, peace and motivation for all you do. Do not look back and be fearful for anything.

Allow a thought system that you richly deserve to be established in your consciousness. Let the angels help you to let go of all that no longer sustains you in your life. Acknowledge that the riches of the universe are already present in your life each day; realise this deep within yourself. Do not feel disappointed or rejected if things do not come straight away.

So begin – ask for what it is that you want in your life, always remembering that God, the source of all supply, is already dwelling within you. Trust the process and it will come; do not be put off when negative thoughts appear, turn them around once again into positive ones, saying, 'I Am, I Am, I Am ...'

Always be open-minded about what you want, and let the flow of positive energy work through your requests. Always have faith and know that God dwells within, so believe that what we have asked for is already there, even though there may be no visible results. What you are doing is creating your requests within your reality, so that they will manifest into your physical world, manifest as aspects of God.

You have got to feel them, see them and love them, and believe that your life is always filled with the abundance of the universe, with the abundance of God.

When we ask the angels to help with our requests we know that there is another tool that we can use to create those things that we need in our lives, and that is our imagination. Our imagination can be a great tool in our development. This is where we travel into a world that is positive; this is where our minds create the reality that is already present within us.

When we were children our imagination played an important part in our lives. We were able to journey into a world where we created a totally different view of the world than the one in which we lived. We could be anything that we wanted to be; we created the people and the places. We had laughter and joy beyond anything that we knew in this world. We felt safe and secure. It was a world where we had everything.

As we grew older, that world of imagination seemed to no longer exist. Our thoughts began to take us in a different direction, one where the world of make-believe was only for children. As adults, that world was no longer within us so we let it go, burying it deep inside us. But the angels help us to return to that wonderful world. Through our imagination they can take us back again into that world to help us create our own reality. It is there in that world that we once again recapture those feelings of love, joy and laughter. We do not have to recreate childhood fantasies but we can create the life that we would love to have by journeying inwards into that world of imagination.

One of the things that I have learned to believe in is my ability to manifest from the power of my imagination. I remember a time when I was meditating, that as I journeyed inwards into a place of stillness, a place of silence, I began to become aware of many words and pictures that were being given to me. As I journeyed, my mind seemed to journey back to the childhood story of Peter Pan. I was not sure why that story began to surface but I knew from working with the angels that symbolically they were trying to tell me something. When I returned from my meditation I asked my angels what it was they were trying to show me and how it could help. Their answer was that Peter Pan represents the light that radiates out for all to see, the light that keeps us young and joyful. That light teaches us how to journey between our worlds, a world of love and beauty, a world that contains everything that you wish for in your life.

Peter Pan is a child of light, a child of beauty and joy. In his world he travels to many places to find the wisdom and knowledge that he needs to find the secret of eternal youth. His is a wonderful example of how our imagination can help us to manifest abundance in our daily lives.

# IO

# Three Wishes

It was September 2002 and I decided one day to pay my sister Elaine a visit. She lives close to Rosslare Harbour in County Wexford, so I caught a bus from the centre of Dublin down to Wexford, a distance of about 100 miles. It was a journey that I had made many times before and I was looking forward to relaxing on the bus for the two-and-a-half-hour trip.

The day was very pleasant and it was lovely to just sit and watch the country towns go by as the bus made its way down the east coast. However, when we came to an area known as Ferns the bus drew in and stopped for a while. As I looked out of the window I noticed an old graveyard with a low stone wall around it. The area was well tended and I remember thinking to myself how well it looked and what a good job someone was doing in keeping it so nice and tidy.

Then something happened I would never forget until the day I die. Sitting on the low stone wall was a little man, perhaps 18 inches in height! He smiled and winked at me! I rubbed my eyes and looked again; he was still there smiling at me. He was dressed in a grey suit of clothes and his little eyes twinkled and danced. I couldn't get over the perfect detail about him; he was so small yet so perfectly formed.

He had this cheeky air about him, a mischievous air. I began to laugh and I said to myself, 'You can't be real. I must be seeing things.' But then he spoke and I could hear his voice in my head: 'I'm real all right, why don't you get off the bus and come over and have a chat with me?' I was flabbergasted; what on earth was happening to me? I looked at the other people on the bus. Some of them were looking at the old graveyard but none of them seemed to be aware of the unbelievable sight that I was seeing.

One thing I knew for sure, there was no way in the world that I was getting off that bus in the middle of County Wexford to go and have a chat with a little man that resembled, I suppose, a leprechaun. Then I heard his voice again: 'I'm here to grant you three wishes, anything that you desire.' Three wishes, I repeated to myself, now I felt I really had to ask him if he was a leprechaun. I couldn't think of anything more intelligent to say, so I asked.

'It's funny you should ask that question,' he replied. 'I'm not a leprechaun. In fact, I haven't seen one of those in years.'

I really was stuck for words now. I rubbed my eyes again and looked away but when I looked back he was still there with an amused and slightly sympathetic look on his little face.

'Who are you then, and what do you want with me?' I asked him.

'I'm a nature spirit; there are a great many of us around here if you know how and where to look; you're going to meet a lot of my friends in times to come,' he replied.

He now seemed to be enjoying our encounter; he crossed his little legs, closed his eyes and tilted his face slightly upwards as if he were appreciating the feeling of the sun shining on his little face.

'You're here to grant me three wishes, isn't that the kind of thing a leprechaun does?' I asked with a hint of suspicion.

'I told you I don't know anything about leprechauns,' he replied, his tone becoming a little impatient. 'But you should think seriously about your three wishes, it's not everyone who gets to wish, you know.'

Then, without warning, the bus began to pull away from the wall where he sat. I didn't know what to do. I had been so stunned by our initial encounter that I hadn't had time to really consider what was happening but now, as the bus began to move away, I realised that I didn't want to leave this amazing little creature – there was something so magical about him, and about his energy, something totally ethereal and not of this world. The bus picked up speed and all I could do was sit and watch as he became smaller and smaller. He was waving at me.

Strangely, I remember feeling a sense of loneliness as I continued on the remaining part of my bus journey to Elaine's home. This little man, whoever or whatever he was, had left a real impression on me. I recalled his words that I would meet a lot of his friends in times to come and I smiled to myself as I did so. When I reached Elaine's house I couldn't wait to tell her exactly what had happened on the bus journey. She couldn't suppress a laugh when I related the whole story to her, especially when I mentioned the three wishes.

'You're not going to ask him for a pot of gold are you?' she giggled.

It was in my bedroom much later that evening that the little man appeared again and this time he wasn't alone. He had two pixie-like little ladies with him. They were about the same height as him and their energy was wondrous; they sparkled and danced around the room and the atmosphere instantly became filled with a sense of joy and fun. I realised I was overjoyed to see the little man again – and his two companions.

'Welcome back,' I said. 'Who are your two friends?'

'This is Lumar and this is Annie,' he replied.

'They're so beautiful, they're like real little fairies,' I said in wonder, looking at the perfect little figures as they danced around and seemed to be exploring every corner of the room.

'Fairies, yes, I suppose we are fairies in a way, if you want us to be,' said the little man. And with that he drew his hand in an arc above the two little female figures and they immediately stopped their dancing and looked at him, wide-eyed and expectantly. 'I told you that you could have three wishes. You don't have to wish, it's up to you,' he said. I surprised myself at just how quickly I closed my eyes and began to consider my three wishes. Three wishes? What did I really want in my life at that moment, I asked myself? I definitely wanted my connection with the angels to become stronger and stronger, so I wished for that. My son Jason was experiencing difficulty getting a job as an electrician, after spending quite a while training for that career, so I wished that he might get a job. Lastly, it had become a dream of mine that one day I might open a centre in Ireland where people could come and learn about my work with the angels, so I wished for that.

'If it is God's will then so let it be,' said the little man as he drew his arm across the room in another arc. 'But remember what I told you – there are a great many of us if you know where and how to look. May God be with you always.'

With that, all three of the little fairies disappeared. I didn't want them to go, their energy was so beautiful, so sparkling, so intensely alive. That is the feeling I was left with after they disappeared, one of alive-ness, of boundlessness, of pure magic. I can honestly say that even after my encounters with the angel realm what I had experienced with these three little entities was somehow different to anything that had gone before. There was just something about their purity and innocence. These little creatures were the very essence of the joy of being alive.

I spent the next day walking on the beautiful beach at Wexford, close to Elaine's home, but I couldn't get the memory of my three little friends out of my mind so that evening I contacted Angel Anne and asked her about the encounter. She smiled when I told her that the little man had granted me three wishes.

'Three? That's a lot, you're very lucky,' she laughed. 'There are many dimensions and energies in this universe that human beings know nothing of and nature spirits are among them. Humans generally regard them to be a myth, but the thing about myths, legends and fairy tales is that they have a basis in truth. The whole myth of the leprechaun in Ireland grew up around the fact that nature spirits do exist and you will find the people who experienced so-called leprechauns many years ago in Ireland were simple people with a love of the land and a love for each other, but as they related what they had encountered other people created the myth of the leprechaun and it grew and grew.

'You happened to encounter three nature spirits yesterday and it was a beautiful experience. The first thing to do if you want to meet with a nature spirit is to open your heart to them; they are all around you here on earth, especially in places of great beauty like here in Wexford.'

I often see nature spirits now, especially around trees for some reason. I remember sitting by the swimming pool in Spain one day, and as I looked at one of the beautiful palm trees that lined the side of the pool a little nature spirit appeared out from the tree. He had very brown skin and black hair and he did this little dance around the base of the tree. He danced around in a little circle then he would stop and look at the tree as if he wanted me to look more closely at it. When I did look closely I got a fright: there was the face of an Native American Indian in the tree, and as I continued to look his image got stronger and stronger and then he pointed at a house that was about 100 metres from the pool. I could hear his voice in my head: 'I need you to connect with the people in that house; the people there have a strong connection to Native American Indians and I need you to deliver a message for me,' he said.

Then I became aware of the energy of another man, quite elderly, in his seventies perhaps, and I knew that he wasn't long in the spirit world. His energy became very strong, stronger than the Indian's, and I knew that he too had a connection to the house across from the swimming pool.

Now my husband Fran isn't the shy retiring type and when I told him that I had a message for the people who lived in the house he simply went over, introduced himself and explained the situation. When Fran mentioned the Indian appearing in the tree the lady of the house immediately expressed an interest in meeting me.

As I entered the lady's house I became aware of the two energies of the Indian and the elderly man. The Indian didn't say anything; I just explained that he was there and the lady spoke up.

'Oh that's wonderful. I believe I know the relations of that Indian, I've done shamanic work with them on a reservation in Alaska.' As she spoke these words I could see the Indian nod and smile as if to say this was correct but he still didn't say anything. It was the spirit of the elderly man that spoke.

'Do you see that man over there?' he asked, pointing to another elderly man sitting on a chair. 'He's my brother and he's very miserable. He misses me; I only passed over into spirit two months ago and he's still mourning. We were very close; we sailed on navy ships around the world together. Please tell him not to grieve, tell him I'm fine and I really like it here.'

When I relayed this information to the man, the atmosphere in the room totally changed. It became lighter, even joyous; other members of the elderly man's family were also present, including a son and a daughter-in-law, and they began to celebrate the man's passing rather than mourn him. As the joy spread around the room I paused and gave thanks to the little nature spirit who had led me to these people. Without his help I wouldn't have been able to relate this beautiful message at all. Nature spirits' function in this world is through the beauty of Mother

Nature, to bring a sense of joy and wonder into people's lives when they can.

I recall another instance when a nature spirit was responsible for indicating to me that I could be of help to someone. It was a nice summer's day and I was sitting in the garden of my home in Blanchardstown, when I noticed a lovely energy around a number of flowers that I had planted some time ago. As I watched the flowers gently move around in the slight breeze, a little fairy-like creature appeared on top of them and jumped down onto the ground. As with many of the nature spirits I've encountered, she began to do a little dance in front of me. It seems it's their way of telling you they have something to say and their energy seems to increase the more they dance until eventually they impart their message. What happened this time was that the little creature stopped dancing and looked at me. Then I heard a voice say, 'We need help.' That's all it said, so I asked who it was that needed help, but the voice retorted, 'We'll send an email.' Now I thought this was really very strange, as I know nothing about computers and at that time I don't think I was even capable of sending an email; it's not my favourite activity even today. But that was all the voice said and the little fairy hopped back into the flowers and disappeared.

I got on with my day and I didn't give the encounter that much more thought until the next morning, when there was a knock at my door. When I answered it a man, maybe in his mid-thirties, was standing there and behind him was a white van with the words 'Internet access and email' written in bold letters across it. Well, I knew immediately this was the email I was going to receive and I asked him to come in.

He explained to me that he was a telecom engineer, but the tale he related to me wasn't a happy one. He had become estranged from his wife and there had been a long history of both emotional and physical abuse between them. Even though he had separated from his wife and left the family home some time ago, that wasn't the end of the matter. He was now with a new partner but his former wife continued to abuse him and his children had been turned against him. The poor man was very distraught and as we talked the angels began to show me the image of a woman, also somewhere in her thirties. I asked the man if the woman fitted the description of his wife but he said no, it fitted the description of his present partner. I now understood why the voice had said 'we' need help, because the angels were letting me see that this lady's emotional state was even more fragile than that of the man in front of me.

The angels proceeded to show me a history of sexual abuse that this lady had suffered as a young child. This was something she had suppressed until now and once she had become involved in a relationship with the man in front of me it was beginning to bring past memories to the surface. It was also related to me that this lady had not explained to her current partner about her past and what had happened to her. All in all, it was a pretty sad set of circumstances and I must admit that I didn't know what to do or what advice to give this man.

But then Angel Anne flashed into my consciousness and made it very clear to me that I couldn't do anything for this young woman and that she needed to go and see a professional counsellor who specialised in cases of sexual abuse. But she also told me that the man *could* be helped because what he really needed was spiritual nourishment and that he should continue to come and see me. At first I was a little concerned, because I'm very aware that I'm not trained in any professional way to help people. I only see my role as relating what, if anything, the angels have to say to any person who has come to see me. But Angel Anne was adamant that this man should come back and visit me. So I told him the advice I had been given: that his partner must go and seek professional help but that he should come back and visit me again if he so wished.

The man took his leave but he returned three days later. Very often the angels will have some advice for people and once they have given the advice that is the last time they will comment on that person. I don't believe it's that the angels are not interested in the people. Rather, it seems to me, angels say what they have to say and then keep their counsel. They are very aware that human beings have free will and choice and that things must take their natural course here on earth. So, although angels can in certain circumstances intervene in the physical realm, they rarely do. However, something quickly became very evident to me regarding this man. Angel Anne seemed determined to help him and she seemed to know exactly what help it was that he needed. As he began to repeat all his problems to me, she simply said, 'Tell him he needs to become still within.' So I told him.

'I can't be still. My whole world is falling apart around me. I don't know what to do, or where to turn,' he pleaded with me.

'Tell him he doesn't have to turn anywhere; he's in exactly the right place now,' replied Angel Anne gently. As she was saying this, I instinctively knew that this man was going to be around me for some time to come and that there would be a positive resolution to his predicament.

I was running meditation classes from my home at the time and Angel Anne told me to tell the man to attend. I ran the classes twice weekly and this man began to get so much from them he tried to persuade me to put on extra classes so that he could come along more often. As we meditated during those classes I had the most wondrous sight of Angel Anne as she surrounded this man with a beautiful healing light. It seemed to penetrate right into his soul, into his very structure, into his DNA. I knew great change was beginning to take place within him.

Angel Anne also instructed me to dig out an old tape I had by a well-known spiritual counsellor and writer on the importance of forgiveness in everyone's lives.

'That tape was actually written under the guidance of the angels many years ago for people like this man and it reveals the true path to take to get out of his problems,' explained Angel Anne.

One day, after we had finished a meditation class, the man told me that his partner had gone and sought professional help for her problems and although it was tough going, things were beginning to move and healing was taking place. As for the man himself, he was fast becoming a different person. He explained to me that he too had gone to see a counsellor and he was finding it very helpful. But he said that what was of even more help to him was that for the first time in his life he was beginning to slow down and learn to be still within.

'It's as if I've been involved in this race all my life, never knowing why I was racing or where the finish line was; it was all just about the racing,' he said. I believe the importance of inner stillness is an enormously important message for all of us. I know in my own journey with the angels, through the grace of God, it was they who initially kept up the contact with me, as I wasn't still enough within myself to be able to do it at first. But as I grew more and more still I was able to establish a continuous awareness of the angels' presence.

And so it is today. I meditate daily for never less than an hour and sometimes for a lot more. I'm not saying that everyone has to do this, but I do believe we all do need a degree of stillness within ourselves. Somehow we all know that this is right, don't we? There is a part in all of us that is still – it's pure stillness – it's God. It may be buried very deep inside some of us but it is there; all we need to do is to consciously contact it.

I could give you more examples of how little nature spirits, or you could call them fairies, have helped me to communicate messages of hope and joy to different people. They are part of the beauty of Mother Nature and they have the ability to communicate with us and share with us the healing elements of Mother Nature.

When you are out in the countryside, just pause for a moment and appreciate the wonderful fields, trees, rivers and even waterfalls that surround you. Become still and really sense that they are alive; everything around you is alive – just let their true essence become a part of you, then you will be close to communicating with the nature spirits.

It may be tempting to think of nature spirits or fairies as being a total invention that only exists in people's imagination. However, the truth is they are elements of nature with intelligence beyond anything we can begin to know. I remember gazing one day at this lovely big tree; it was enormous – perhaps 50 feet high and possibly hundreds of years old. I remember thinking to myself what kind of intelligence must be present in this tree to allow it to grow up so majestically and beautifully over all those years without any help whatsoever from man? That is the very same intelligence that nature spirits possess.

If you wish to really connect with nature spirits or the fairy kingdom your intentions at all times must be honourable and true. When you show love and compassion in your heart for the fairy element, they will begin to slowly come toward you in your life. Perhaps for many of you the most convenient place to connect with nature spirits is in your own garden, if you are lucky enough to have a garden.

I used to love to get out in my garden in Dublin just to sit there quietly and slowly let the nature spirits reveal themselves to me in that mischievous, gentle, sparkling way of theirs. If you are tending your garden and wish to make it a place where you can communicate with them, invite them to be with you so they can show you what it is you must do. Fairies and nature spirits are very loving and very gentle. Every time you are tending your garden call on them and let them slowly illuminate the world of Mother Nature that is all around you.

Needless to say, nature spirits are very concerned with the way we treat our planet – Mother Earth – they essentially *are* Mother Earth. Today a great many people are being influenced by nature spirits, whether they know it or not. Nature spirits are influencing people who have a great interest in our environment and who want to keep our earth safe and clean from dangerous toxins that are being put into it every day.

If you have a real concern for the many different species of animals that live on planet earth or if you are concerned about the vast number of life forms that exist in our oceans and that are being unconsciously destroyed by mankind every day, you too are being influenced by nature spirits.

Maybe you have had a sudden urge to become involved with an organisation like Greenpeace or some other organisation in your area that campaigns to protect animals. This too is the nature spirits at work in your subconscious. You may feel moved to write to different governments around the world on how you feel about the injustice that surrounds many issues that affect our planet.

If you sometimes think that it's all a bit too much for you, because you are only one person and one person can't make a real difference to the many global problems facing planet earth today, then think again. Get out into the countryside among Mother Nature and ask the nature spirits to guide you; ask them to make themselves real to you. Once you have made that wondrous connection you will realise that you do make a difference. You will realise that you, the nature spirits, the fairies and Mother Nature are all one – one in the same God.

# I I

# A World of Spirit

The angels go to great lengths to demonstrate to me that this world of ours is in fact a world of timeless spirit. In this world of timeless spirit the past, present and future really do not exist, although they appear to be very real indeed.

An incident occurred not that long ago that dramatically brought home to me the fact that the world of spirit can overcome time and space and impose itself very dramatically on the physical plane when it so wishes.

A journalist from Dublin phoned me in Spain and asked me to look at certain photographs that were taken at a recent commemoration ceremony for the victims of the Stardust disaster in Dublin in 1981. All Irish people of a certain age will remember the deep sadness and distress that surrounded the events that occurred at the Stardust discotheque in the Artane district of north Dublin on 14 February 1981. The venue caught fire and, despite valiant efforts on the part of the fire service and people present, forty-eight young people were trapped in the burning building and lost their lives.

What followed was a deeply traumatic time for the relatives of the people who perished and, despite a tribunal of inquiry and police investigation, it was never possible to conclude what exactly had been the cause of the fire. The disaster will remain forever lodged in the consciousness of the Irish people.

However, the relatives of those who died took grave exception to the tribunal's verdict that the most probable cause of the fire was arson and years and years of dispute and conflict ensued between the families of those who were lost and the authorities. But then, in February 2009, approaching the twenty-eighth anniversary of the disaster, the Irish Government agreed to strike the tribunal's verdict from the parliamentary record.

I'm very aware that I can't speak in any way for the families who had lost their loved ones. I can't even begin to imagine the pain those poor people must have endured through the years as the controversy dragged on concerning the exact cause of that dreadful fire. But I feel I'm right in saying that this decision by the Government was greeted with a sense of relief and with hope that even after such a very long time there might yet be a further thorough inquiry.

The journalist from Dublin had sent me a series of photographs that were taken outside the scene of the tragedy in Artane, as a commemoration service was under way for the forty-eight victims. Of course, I wasn't present at the service, but apparently numerous people had commented on the night that a deep sense of peace, unlike anything that had previously been encountered at other commemoration services for the departed, was palpable on this night.

One of the relatives told me it was a very still night and as the names of those who had lost their lives were read out over forty-eight lit candles could be seen to really move about and flicker as if an unseen power was influencing them. But what was really remarkable about these photographs is that they contained what appeared to be some very unusual and unexplained phenomena. As a group of the relatives of those who lost their lives stood in prayer over the candles, a shaft of unexplained light can be clearly seen coming down from above and resting on the group.

When I first looked at this photograph what immediately flashed into my consciousness was the term 'the bridge of souls'. I could also sense the souls of some of the people who had been lost in this terrible fire, but what I was sensing was a feeling of joy and of release. Another photograph that was taken on that night contained something truly amazing, something that I found totally humbling. In this particular picture, of one the relatives who was also a survivor from the fire, I could make out the image of a young girl to her right and just below her face it is possible to discern the image of a small angel, complete with wings. The girl whose photograph I was looking at later confirmed to me that her younger sister had indeed perished in the fire, as had another sister.

As I continued to look at the series of photographs, there must have been six or seven of them, I began to get the image of an elderly man. The more I looked at the photographs the stronger his energy became, but I knew that this man had not actually died in the fire. Rather, his family believes that stress and a broken heart had led to his death from cancer. And, sure enough, it was confirmed to me that this poor man was the father of the two young girls who had died that fateful night in north Dublin.

I am told that several well-known photographers had looked at the photographs but they couldn't account for the unusual phenomena that could be clearly seen on several of the prints. Apparently there is an occurrence known as 'lens flare' that can happen on photographs. I've never heard of the term before, and I really couldn't tell you anything about it, but it was mentioned to me as being a possible cause for the unexplained lights and images that can be seen on the photographs. All I can tell you is what I felt when I saw the photographs, and that was a feeling of release and of joy. I sensed that those souls that perished so tragically in the fire so long ago were now finally free, and they desperately wanted their loved ones to know that. So desperately that I believe they were able to manifest that desire into the physical realm, into the photographs, so demonstrating that we truly do live in a world of spirit.

It may sound a fantastic notion to some of you, but it is by no means the first time I've come across the world of spirit making an impression on the physical plane. I only hope and pray that the loved ones involved in this terrible tragedy, who have suffered for so long, may now be able to find rest, just as those whom they have lost are now doing. May they rest in peace.

The physical realm of time and space is no barrier to the angels when they wish to convey something to me. This was first brought home dramatically to me when I received a call one evening from America. The caller, a lady from Pittsburgh, told me her name and explained to me that she had got my number from a friend of hers who had visited me when she was on holiday in Ireland.

When she mentioned her friend's name I immediately remembered the lady in question, as the angels had given me a lovely message for her and she was delighted with what they had to tell her. This lady had obviously gone home to America and mentioned me to her friend, who had then decided to phone me up. The remarkable thing was that as I spoke to this lady it was as if she was sitting in front of me and the angels were letting me know a great many details concerning her and her loved ones. The angels were actually providing a clear channel of communication and all those thousands of miles across the Atlantic Ocean between us meant nothing, nothing at all. The angels are always demonstrating to me, in so many different ways, that this is not our world with all its rules, physical limitations and appearances. No, rather this is God's world, a world of spirit in which many things arise and take on appearances.

Human beings arise and take on an appearance. We appear to be made of a solid body, one of flesh and blood, bones and muscle. However, that is only an appearance; we are actually spiritual beings made of God – that is really the truth! The angels go to great trouble to bring this beautiful truth home to me time and time again and I believe it holds the secret as to how to live our lives successfully. If you can hold to this universal truth then all things are possible.

Suppose you have a problem with your body. Let's say it's with your lungs; you immediately bring to mind that although in the human sense you have two physical lungs, they are really made of spirit, a spirit that is perfect and immaculately whole and healthy. Now, although the

physical body may be testifying to a physical problem with
your lungs, you just hold to the divine realisation that all
is perfect in spirit and that includes your lungs. A great
many people have healed themselves simply by knowing
this universal truth and by then applying it.

The angels are always demonstrating to me that this is
God's world, a spiritual world and we are all children of
God. They just seem to love to show me that there are no
boundaries between God and us, we only imagine that
there are and our minds seem to love to keep these imag-
inary boundaries in place. The mind always wants to be
'king of the castle', but there is only one king of the castle
and that's God. I remember one evening while on holiday,
in a restaurant in Torrevieja in southern Spain, when the
angels chose a remarkable and lovely way of demonstrating
that the world of spirit entertains no boundaries between
God and us. Fran and I had spent a lovely afternoon just
walking around the town of Torrevieja, browsing and doing
a bit of window-shopping.

One of the great bonuses of holidaying in Spain is that
eating out is cheap, especially compared to Ireland. I sometimes think that everything, anywhere, is cheap compared
to Ireland, but that's another story! On that evening in
Torrevieja we decided we would go to a little restaurant
that we knew and have our evening meal there rather than
have to cook. When we arrived at the restaurant we were
greeted by the owner who showed us to a table by the
window. The restaurant was very full and there were a great
many different nationalities present, tourists from all over
Europe and even further afield.

At some of the tables beside us there was a party of

perhaps a dozen people and they were having a great time as they chatted and laughed and enjoyed their food and wine. I commented to Fran that the young girl whose twenty-first birthday they were celebrating was very pretty. Fran looked at me blankly and said, 'How do you know that they're celebrating her birthday?' I looked at him, laughed and said, 'Well I can hear them, everyone can hear them, and they're quite loud.'

'Yes,' replied Fran, 'but they're talking in German and you don't understand German.'

'Don't be so ridiculous,' I said. 'They're talking in English. I can clearly hear them; they're waiting for the girl's brother to come in, they think he may have got lost and can't find the restaurant.' Just as I said these words a young lad of about eighteen came into the restaurant to be greeted by a big cheer from the party.

'See?' I said to Fran rather smugly. But he wasn't really interested in the young lad's arrival; he was looking at me dumbfounded.

'You can actually hear all those people speaking in English?' he asked.

'What are you talking about?' I replied. 'Of course I can hear them talking in English; they are talking in English.'

'They're not, you know, they're all talking in German. I haven't been able to make out a word any of them has said since we came in,' he said. Then he pointed to a couple seated to the other side of us, away from the birthday party.

'What language are they speaking?' he asked. I looked at the couple, whom I could clearly hear discussing the best route to take out of Torrevieja to drive to Alicante.

'Well, they're talking in English too. I can hear them,

they're discussing what's the shortest way to Alicante,' I said, smiling at Fran. He just looked at me and shook his head.

'They're not,' he said, laughing now. 'They either Swedish or Dutch and there's no way that they're speaking in English.'

We both had to laugh about this incredible experience, which the angels were letting me have for some reason. So when we got home that evening I spoke to them and asked why they had let me experience what had happened in the restaurant. It was Angel Anne who provided me with the answer.

'We've told you many, many times before that God's world is the world of spirit and in that world there are no boundaries and no restrictions,' she explained. 'It is a world of wholeness, of perfection, of oneness. In your human world, with all its apparent rules, laws, causes and effects, things like different languages are necessary for people to exist. But not so in God's world, where all is already one. We just thought we'd demonstrate that fact for you in the restaurant. It was quite fun, wasn't it?' And she was right; it had been fun and very remarkable. Once again I felt so privileged to be able to appreciate what the angels were conveying to me – that all is well, we are all children of God, an integral part of his glorious world, which is already perfectly whole.

Harmony already *is*, all we need to do is to burst the bubble that we surround ourselves with, the bubble of doubts, thoughts and emotions that can appear to keep us at an arm's length from God. We need to burst that bubble, to pierce that veil, then we will realise that harmony already is. Our purpose here in this human world as children of God is to demonstrate God, to demonstrate that he is a living, moving being in our life and the angels are on hand to help us do just that. These wonderful creatures of pure light are right there beside us, closer to us than our breath, ready to help us in any way they can, ready to help us to realise our true identity – that of children of God.

Something that has been brought home very strongly to me over the past few years is just how much the angels can and do influence people and events around the world. After you have made a personal connection with your own angel you too will begin to see where and when the angels are actually influencing people and events right around our entire planet. It's an amazing experience to watch certain people as they go about their jobs or professions and to know that the angels are guiding and influencing them, whether they are aware of it or not.

I personally have seen the angels take an interest in and become involved with show-business people, sports people, politicians and religious leaders; it doesn't matter who or what you are, the angels are interested in you.

Sometimes I may be listening to the radio and a song will come on that I have never heard before, but I will know instinctively that the angels had a part in writing it, even if the songwriter wasn't aware of their presence when it was written.

Of course, human beings will never actually *be* angels and yet here on earth there are many humans with angelic qualities. I suppose they could be referred to as earthbound angels. There are many people who have great compassion, peace, understanding and kindness towards their fellow men and they seek no rewards. Have you at some time in your life met somebody who touched you by his or her mere presence?

It happened to me about two years ago. I was giving an angel workshop in a place called Hønefoss in Norway when I met what I can only describe as a 'holy man'. His energy was extraordinary; it's no exaggeration to say that he radiated divinity. When he entered the room I suddenly felt totally humbled to be in his presence. A lot of angels I had never encountered before, that were connected to this man, suddenly appeared in the room. He was in his early thirties and I would guess he had no idea that there was anything remotely special about him at all.

He was involved in healing and I could sense that this man's presence was so pure that he had been responsible for healing many people of different ailments. Being in his presence made me feel very humble; he radiated such love and peace and he was in the presence of many remarkable angels.

As I spoke to him, it became even more clear to me that he had no idea of the angelic qualities that were present in him, and yet all who came in contact with him were touched by his presence. A lot of people commented on it immediately after he left the room. I will never forget him, as he touched my heart and soul in a special way; there was a great innocence about him.

There will always be people who will walk this earth with these angelic qualities; they have been truly touched by the light of God that dwells within them.

In my journey with the angels I have met many people,

including children, who have this angelic presence. People in all walks of life, some of them very well-known people who appear regularly on television or in movies. Others whose life revolves around politics – they all carry this light from God within and very often they have no conscious awareness of it at all.

One hugely positive message I have received from the angels recently is that a new breed of politician is slowly emerging here on the earth. For the first time in world history politicians are appearing that have only the best interests of the people at heart, although this may take some time before it becomes clear due to what has gone before in political terms. The angels have explained to me that people's prejudices are being pushed aside and this is being reflected politically; slowly a new vision is emerging for all of us.

That vision is of a world where people can come together without any injustice to each other. The possibility is emerging of a more peaceful, safe and better world for all. It will be a world without fear, with free movement for all, a world where people can be equal no matter what the colour of their skin or the place that they come from, a world where people can unite to live in harmony beside each other. The angels have told me that the Middle East will be the common ground where it will start, however unlikely that may appear at the moment.

There are many people around the world who strive to make a difference in people's lives and the energy of the angels is very much with them, guiding them and helping them where and when they can. There are people who work with the sick and the dying, who give their time voluntarily to try and bring a little comfort to others. They do not look for rewards or recognition for what they do; their purpose is to help people in time of great need and they just feel compelled to do that. There are numerous examples – high-profile people like Mother Teresa, Nelson Mandela and Martin Luther King are all classic examples of what I am talking about.

Then there are all our doctors and nurses and volunteers. The angels made it clear to me that volunteering is something that all of us could do more of, especially in these recessionary times when people are losing their jobs. If we have to spend a period without employment, what better way to get through it than to volunteer to do something for others?

The energy of the angels is very much behind organisations like the Hospice Foundation and the Red Cross. Both these bodies are great examples of just what can be achieved when people truly give. Just look around at all the wonderful humanitarian workers there are throughout the world. They do make a real difference, this cannot be denied, and you can too. You too can have angelic qualities while here on earth; you can become an earthbound angel. It could be that you simply take time to listen to someone who is going through a difficult time in their life. If we are honest with ourselves we probably all know someone who is going through a rough patch. Or perhaps you could be there for a family member or friend when they need a shoulder to lean on? Always remember that the simplest of tasks can make a difference in someone else's life.

Remember that angels always have a great understanding

of you and what is going on in your life. Don't wait for the angels to come and give you some good task to do; rather, go out and do the good task anyway. If you can do this you will find that the energy of the angels is already with you as you perform your good task – you will have made that angelic connection. Angels don't come to live your life for you – they can't do that. They come to assist you and to help you to find a positive solution to the problems that you and the people around you may be facing.

In all of life, down through the history of time, there have always been people who walk this earth with angelic qualities. They come from all walks of life, each with a common bond or a vision to reach out and to help people. They bring peace and harmony – no one person can really be singled out because each individual is part of a wider collective consciousness reaching out to help mankind.

Those who look after the sick and dying are good examples of people doing the angels' bidding while here on earth. So too are the humanitarian workers who help out in different parts of the world. Then there are the peacekeepers who try to make the world a better place for all of us to live in peace and harmony.

Children who become carers in our society deserve a special mention. There are a great many of them who step up and perform the task of an adult by taking care of their family's needs. They can sometimes be recognised by a serenity and a wisdom that glows from inside them and a maturity far, far beyond their years. The truth is that if we look around us people with angelic qualities are everywhere; it can be your friend, your neighbour or the stranger you meet in the street. Of course, in order to become an earthbound angel it is necessary for us to allow the angels' energy to reach us, to allow that world of positive thought to become more and more a reality for us each day.

So sit back, be as still as you can and let the angels help you to learn to train your thoughts away from negative thinking and into a more positive way of living and learning. Watch as the angels show you that your thoughts are powerful and that what you think, feel and say can create your reality, leading you into an area where your lives can be more balanced and centred in everything you do and in how you treat others. Watch, as you become earthbound angels.

# 12

# This Cruel World

I was in the kitchen of my home in Blanchardstown one evening, when the image of a gun suddenly flashed before me. It was a small black weapon with a brown wooden handle, rather like the guns you see strapped to detectives' hips on TV police shows. The image was so vivid and clear that I immediately knew it was important and that I should pay very close attention.

More information quickly followed. I was told that one of the two men coming to visit me that evening was carrying the gun in his back pocket and that he was intent on carrying out a revenge shooting for his friend who had recently been executed in a shooting incident in Dublin.

Naturally I was shocked by the revelation, the fact that people – mostly young men – are getting shot in Dublin and other Irish cities on almost a daily basis is something that seldom seems to be out of the news these days. Yet I knew that I would be perfectly safe in the company of the two men who were due at my home in less than half an hour.

The car drew right up our driveway to the front door and I had to reassure my husband Fran that everything would be all right when the men entered our home. They were both big individuals, in their late-twenties I would guess, and from Dublin's central inner city area. The man I had been told had the gun sat down in front of me. I had never seen him in my life before. He seemed edgy and ill at ease.

Suddenly, a mass of light blue energy started to form at his left side and I knew that Angel Anne was about to manifest. She instructed me to tell the man that I knew he had a gun in his back pocket. He was stunned.

'But I'm not going to use it on you,' he replied when I informed him I was aware of the weapon.

'I know you're not,' I said. 'I don't know what would happen to you if you tried, but I know I'm completely safe around you.' The man then seemed to relax a little and Anne then set about revealing his life's background to me. Towards the end of the revelation Anne made me aware of a small blond boy, not yet one year old. The boy was the man's son, whom he loved dearly, and Anne kept relaying more and more information about the child to me that I in turn relayed to the man. I could see that the more I concentrated on the young boy the more upset the man was becoming.

'Anne is making it quite clear to me that if you go ahead and carry out your revenge attack you will be separated from your son for a very long time,' I said. 'She's also showing me a circle of never-ending violence that will continue for a long time if you don't stop and consider your actions.' As Anne finished her 'reading' of the man he got up, came across and hugged me. He was now visibly upset and crying.

'My God I don't know how you've done what you've just done, but you've made me stop and think, stop and think about everything,' he sobbed. The man and his friend then left my home and disappeared into the night. I don't know what happened after they left or if the man carried out his attack, but I know Angel Anne did her best to point out to him the consequences of his actions and hopefully he was sufficiently touched not to resort to violence. I hadn't really had the time but what I would really have liked to emphasise to him was the fact that everyone has an angel that is concerned solely with that person; it doesn't matter who you are, what you do or what you have done in the past. We all have our own personal angels just waiting for us to make contact with them. These angels are commonly referred to as guardian angels.

This universe is run by a series of natural laws and one of the most important laws that pertain to human beings is that we all have free will. So, as with the man mentioned above, Angel Anne could only point out to him the consequences of his actions, but she couldn't prevent him from going out and doing whatever he decided to do – he had free will. Angels can only do things in their way and in their time, they cannot do things in our way and our time. Laws bind them too.

The man with the gun and his friend had heard about me from someone else who had visited me previously and given them my name. The angels have made it very clear to me that I should never judge anyone – they never do. They have also explained to me that I would from time to time encounter people who were involved in some very negative activities, and these people would visit me because they were attracted to the light of the angels, whether they knew it or not.

So it has proved on several occasions that I have had visits from people who were involved in some very negative activities indeed. So negative, in fact, that the room would turn a very dull grey or even black colour when they entered. Some play-acted or pretended they were not really interested in the angels' message, but underneath it all I could sense the fact that they were indeed attracted to the light of the angels. The angels also explained that I should never feel afraid when in their presence, I was protected at all times.

The scourge of drugs and the violence that goes with that business makes me feel very sad and I've watched as Dublin has become a more and more dangerous place to be as a result of this activity. There have been occasions when I have been drawn into the whole tragic side of that murky underworld, but through the grace and love of the angels I've sometimes been able to offer people a little light, sometimes not.

A young man, he couldn't have been more than twenty-two or twenty-three years old, came to visit me once. It was funny but as he sat in front of me the first thing I could see was a big block of wood – nothing else, just this big block of wood; the image would not go away. I could also sense that he was in quite a dilemma, as he was involved in the world of drugs, but not totally involved. I could sense that for this young man there was still a choice to be made; he could still turn his life around if he really wanted to.

As I sat talking to him, I liked him, although I could sense all the negativity that surrounded him and the people with whom he associated. As we were talking, I became aware of another young man who had entered my consciousness. He was roughly the same age as the young man with me and I could sense that the two were very close before he had passed away. Sadly, his passing had been a very violent one. He had been shot – executed – by people who were supposed to have been his friends.

The angels were letting me see exactly what had happened to this man. He had become involved with drugs from an early age, as a lot of the other young people from around their area had done. However, this young man had risen quite quickly in the drugs underworld: a gang had sprung up around him and he had begun to make a lot of money from drugs. When I explained to the young man that I had his friend with me he brightened up. However, his friend, who had passed to the light, was in no mood for niceties.

'He's telling me that you really need to stop and think about where you're going in your life. He says it's not too late to stop, but if you don't there's a good chance that you will end up the same as he did – dead.' I relayed it as it was relayed to me. I could sense and see that all this was very difficult for this young man to hear and take in. I felt that the struggle for him was with the drugs themselves rather than the gang culture and money that was involved in the selling of drugs. Then I asked him a question: 'Can you tell me why the angels have been showing me a large piece of wood since you entered the room?'

'Well, yeah, I suppose I can. It's because I like wood; I used to carve a bit of wood years ago,' he replied with a slight shrug of his shoulders.

'I think you did a bit more than carve a bit of wood.

The angels are showing me a lot of people looking at your carvings and being very impressed,' I said. At this point the man's friend who had passed on came in again.

'I remember his carvings when we were at school. He was absolutely great and he can get back into it if he really wants to,' he enthused. I told the young man what his friend was saying and I told him that was exactly what the angels were saying too.

'Your gift with wood can be your way out of your problems, but you are going to have to have a bit of faith in yourself and allow it to happen,' I told him. 'The angels say the first thing you need to do is to remove yourself from the drugs. If you need help to do that, you must go out and get the help, then things will begin to change for you.'

We talked for a little longer then the young man thanked me and took his leave. As I watched him go out the door I wished there was more that I could do for him, but as he left the sense that it was in no way over for him came back to me and I closed my eyes and wished him well.

The angels had explained to me that from time to time I would encounter people who were involved in the underworld. However, this was brought home to me in a way that I could never have imagined or even dreamed of.

There's a certain road in north Dublin that residents of the area will know, as it runs between the two suburbs of Blanchardstown and Finglas. I used to use it quite a lot as it was a handy shortcut for me, but every time I travelled on it I'd get a very uneasy feeling. Sometimes it would nearly be a feeling of panic at a certain spot on the road.

One evening, I was driving by myself on the road when a young man in his mid-twenties suddenly materialised beside me in the front of the car. I nearly crashed but succeeded in bringing the car to a stop. He sat beside me in a very panicked state. Blood stained his head, hands and most of his shirt. He gripped the dashboard of the car and stared out wild-eyed in terror as if someone was after him. As I looked on in shock, another scene began to unfold in front of my eyes. There were a great many policemen present, some of them in uniform and others with red and orange bibs on as they ran about. I could hear orders being shouted loudly: 'Armed police!' 'Throw down your weapon!' 'Keep still!' There was total confusion, with people ducking and diving. Then I heard shots ring out, there were three or four of them then things went quiet.

Now I could see an ambulance and a priest and lot of people looking on from behind a yellow tape. Then there was just this eerie silence, until I was brought back to my car by the young man, who was still in my front seat looking out the window and all around him, frozen in absolute terror. As I looked at him my eyes began to well up with tears. He was about the same age as my son Jason and, of course, he was some mother's son. What a waste, what an absolute waste of a young life, I thought to myself. As I looked at him certain things became clear to me. This was not the first time he had been engaged in this type of activity; I had the feeling it was like a career for him but this time his luck had run out. He had confronted the police when he was cornered after a robbery and he had been shot. As I continued to look at him, I also had a sense of what it is that drives these young men to commit these types of crimes. There's a certain energy to it, a machismo and a bravado that, when you look behind it, doesn't stand up – it's false. Unfortunately, it's a very strong energy and as he sat in my car and stared out at the world in a terror only he could know I closed my eyes and spoke to the angels.

'Whatever this man has done he has now passed from this earth and I ask you to comfort him now in any way that you can,' I prayed. And as quickly as he had appeared he disappeared and I was left alone in my car by the side of the road.

I know many people will say, 'Good riddance, that's one more criminal off the streets,' when they hear of a case like that of this young man. But I've seen the terrible pain and hurt that these young men leave behind for their loved ones when they choose to get involved in drugs and violence.

A woman once visited me and asked if I could tell her anything about her son, who had been shot in west Dublin in a drugs gang feud. When I contacted the spirit world the young man eventually came through to me. At once, I had the awful sensation of an injury to the back of my head; it was a massive injury, truly awful, as if the back of my head was literally missing. The young man asked me to tell his mother that he was sorry for the hurt he had caused her and if he could turn back time he would and he loved his mother and the rest of his family. His mother became overwhelmed with grief when I related this information to her. But something happened then that took me completely by surprise: another young man appeared in the form of spirit and he looked very similar in appearance to the first young man. I asked him who he was.

'I'm his brother,' he replied, pointing to the first young man. I was then given an image of this young man dying a very violent death, also related to the sale of drugs. I then asked the woman in front of me if she had another son who had passed over. She began to tremble and all the poor lady could do was nod her head. It must have been one of the sorriest sights I had ever encountered, here on earth or in the spirit world – these two young men, somewhere in their mid- to late-twenties, who should have been starting their own families or just out enjoying life, were with me in the world of spirit, asking for their mother's forgiveness and regretting the path they had chosen in their lives.

It's difficult to explain what I feel when I'm with someone from the spirit world and they have a message for a loved one still here on earth. I don't just receive the words from the person who has passed over but a whole scene can be revealed to me. I can have a sense of other members of their family whom they haven't even mentioned and other events that have taken place in their lives while still on earth. And so it was with these two young men. As they asked for their mother's forgiveness I was being made aware of a bad relationship with their father, but it was their younger sisters' energy that came through very strongly to me. They too really missed their older brothers' presence and were devastated by their deaths. I could see many embarrassing and very hurtful things that were said to them following their brothers' passing.

I know a great many parents would wish for their children

never to witness anything like the scene I'm describing here, but I recall at the time wishing that I could transport that scene to every classroom in Ireland and let young people see the final reality of becoming involved in the world of drugs and crime. I had such a great sense of total frustration at the sheer waste of human life, a waste of something that is meant to be simple and good.

When the mother of those two young men left me I thought of my own two young sons, Jason and Dwayne, who were only slightly younger than that mother's two boys. I felt so sad that I had to contact my best friend Angel Anne. She appeared with her beautiful wings open very wide, and as she came closer she brought me into her wings. Her voice was soft and reassuring and she said, 'Life is good when you let it be, you must learn to just let it be.' I feel her message is so important. Life is good if you can just let it be. When we start to add more and more things to life, whether it's drugs or the need for more and more money, we start to create problems for ourselves.

# 13

# A New Calling

The past three years of my life in Dublin had become more and more involved with the angels. The number of people coming to visit me, wishing to find out more about the angels and their work, had increased enormously and it wasn't uncommon for me to see three or four people every day.

While most people were interested in learning how to make a personal connection with the angels, others came looking for messages from loved ones who had passed on, while others were interested in doing healing work with the help of the angels.

I so enjoyed meeting new people every day and seeing the same people return to me time and time again. There is something contained within the angels' message that makes it a totally joyous experience to relate it to others. Indeed, my experience has been that you have to pass it on to others: it's meant to be passed on because it's already ours, we've just unfortunately forgotten a lot of it.

Even though I was hugely enjoying meeting new people and helping them in any way I could I also had something on my mind. It was a matter of great importance to me and I knew it would also affect Fran and my family. I decided I would discuss it with Fran on a short holiday to Spain that we had planned.

It was a beautiful May day and we were walking on the beach at Santiago de la Ribera near Orihuela Costa in the south of Spain on the third day of our week's holiday. We had bought a small house in Orihuela Costa some years previously, mainly because we wanted a place to bring the kids during the holidays. There weren't that many other people on the beach, as the tourist season hadn't really kicked in, but it was a perfect day, not too warm and not a cloud to be seen in a clear blue sky.

However, as we walked I was in a pensive mood. I had something important to tell Fran and I wasn't at all sure how he was going to react to it. My relationship with the angels was growing and growing, with new angels introducing themselves to me all the time. While I was reporting a lot of what was happening back to Fran I knew he was still having a hard time accepting all of it.

Looking back, he was a solid rock of support for me throughout my illness and his interest in the presence of the angels and their abilities had definitely increased with time, but I felt there was a large part of him that was still sceptical about the whole phenomenon. I knew it had been especially hard for him at the beginning of my illness when I first started to witness the people moving around in front of me in my bedroom. He had commented to me more than once about how I had turned on all the lights and the fact that the house had been lit up like a Christmas tree each evening when he returned from work – it had clearly annoyed him. I could also see that immediately after my illness, when I was spending so much time in my meditation room communicating with the angels, this also sometimes irked him. I was also aware that Fran couldn't possibly have understood all the messages I was receiving from the angel realm, although I did my best to share some of them with him; even I didn't understand them all! And now the time had come to tell him something that I knew would shock him. As we strolled hand in hand by the ocean I spoke up.

'The angels have made a request of me, well no, they've actually made a request of both of us, but I'm very worried about how you're going to handle it,' I said hesitantly.

'Come on, out with it,' said Fran with a slight frown.

'Well, the angels have asked me to move to Spain permanently,' I said. 'They say I can't do their work properly back in Dublin and I need to get away. They say it won't be forever but I do need to move and I can't move unless you come with me.' I had rather blurted it out.

'Why do we have to move?' asked Fran. 'How can we move? Do you want me to sell the house in Dublin? And what about the boys?' he asked, really frowning now. It was all true. In order to move to Spain we would have to sell our house in Dublin because we had no funds, and for our two sons who were in their late teens the attraction of Spain was beginning to wear a bit thin. They wanted to be with their mates and girlfriends back in Dublin and would have no interest in a new life in Spain. As I stood on that beach in the warm May sunshine it all seemed to be impossible and I felt dejected. At that moment a voice uttered these words in my head: "Tell Fran he will become your eyes and ears while you work for us; tell him he will receive a sign.' The voice stopped me in my tracks. It had an authority about it; it was as if what it had said had already come true. I also recalled that Angel Anne had told me months ago that the angels would deliver a sign to Fran. I repeated what the voice said to Fran. He looked at me and I could see he really wanted to believe but it was still a little too much for him; but now I knew that he was going to receive a sign.

It was on the last night of our holiday that Fran got his sign. We had retired early to bed because we had an early start the next day to catch a flight back to Dublin. We had set the alarm for 6am but I woke before it went off to find that Fran wasn't in the bed beside me. I thought he must be down in the kitchen making a cup of tea, so I got dressed and went down.

Fran was sitting on our small settee in the front room just staring straight ahead of him. When he saw me he got up and came over and hugged me.

'Oh my God,' he said. 'It's true, it's all true.' I looked at him and asked what had happened.

'Last night, I don't know what time it was, I woke up and I was looking ahead of me when I saw an orb of light appear at the end of the room, then another one appeared and then a third one. They were about the size of tennis balls.' He related the information with a look of total wonder in his eyes. 'Then they formed into one bigger orb and it came right up in front of me. I didn't feel scared, I felt overjoyed. I knew it meant me no harm and then a voice said, "Trust in us" and the orb just faded away,' he explained. He also explained that he had prayed to the angels and asked them to send him a sign because he was fearful of the future and what it might bring.

I know that those orbs of light were sent by the angels to give Fran the faith he needed to help me do the angels' work. I know this in the same way that I know that if anyone has enough faith in the angels to just stand back and take themselves out of the picture they are just left with God. This is very important – you must remove yourself from the scene because it's yourself that is blocking the connection with the angels and if you can remove yourself you are just left with the angels and God. What God wants will then become clear to you.

On the flight back to Dublin that morning it was a different Fran beside me and we were already making plans on how we would move full time to Spain. And that's exactly what we did: we sold our house, we rented an apartment for the boys, who were now with steady girlfriends and out working anyway and weren't in the slightest bit worried about us going off to Spain, and on 31 June 2005 we moved permanently to Spain.

It soon became very clear to me why the angels had asked me to make the move. Angels can materialise at any time or any place that they choose to. They can relate messages to human beings here on earth at any time they want to, but I've found that it is only in deep quiet and silence that they will impart a lot of their wisdom and knowledge. Spain turned out to be the perfect place for me to find that quiet and silence. Looking back now, I was also very much tied up with my family in Dublin at the time and I don't believe I would have been able to knuckle down and devote the amount of time necessary to do what the angels were asking of me.

In Spain I quickly developed a routine whereby I would rise in the morning and go into meditation for a number of hours and the angels would communicate with me. I would also meditate in the afternoons. I soon realised that there would also be a lot of writing involved in my work with the angels. I was never the most brilliant student in school – to tell you the truth I was delighted when I left school at the age of sixteen, I couldn't wait to get out the door! So as the angels related their wisdom to me I had no option but to take it down in long hand and then, thanks to a neighbour who happened to be a school-teacher, I would get it all typed up and spell-checked. It was a long, laborious process but the angels' message always remained intact and correct and that was all that concerned me. It still is all that concerns me to this day.

When I say that my work with the angels involved a lot of writing, among the information they had relayed to me was a work called *A Practical Guide To Working With Angels and Spirit Guides.* This is a guide that I have gone on to use in my own angel workshops and it is remark-able how many people it has benefited. Another very important piece of work was entitled *A Guide To Healing With Angels*, which is a dialogue between myself and a number of angels who specialise in healing. There was also *A Book of Inspirational Messages From the Angels*, *An Angelic Philosophy For The World* and a great many poems. So you can see what I mean when I say I was kept busy with the writing!

It was becoming more and more clear to me why the angels had asked me to move to Spain, but I still had some doubts in my heart and they sometimes really troubled me. I recall one morning sitting down in my meditation room feeling very troubled and speaking to God. When I invoke the Kingdom of Heaven and I am in the presence of God something miraculous happens; it's difficult to explain in words but there is a feeling of immaculate wholeness, of oneness. All questions a human being might have about who they are or why they are here on this earth are answered during these times; they are not answered in words, they are answered by this wholeness – it is immaculately whole and it is eternal. But it was a troubled Francesca who went to God that morning in Spain. This is exactly what I said to the Father:

O my Lord, there are many aspects of my life that I do not understand at this moment. Have I chosen the wrong way to take me to a place where I feel I do not belong?

Have I thrown away everything that you have shown me in the short space of time that we have been journeying together? Have I lost my way totally, lost in a place that does not feel like home to me? Will my spirit fade away, leaving me standing still, not knowing the way forward? Caught in a place not knowing if the voice of spirit is calling me or failing me.

What is it that I am supposed to do, to fulfil my journey with you? A journey that you opened up to me, to find my way, to find my light, my true existence, my purpose and to find who I truly am. Will you tell me or will you let me walk in my shadow wondering if everything I do is wrong?

What is it that I must see to help me gain the knowledge that I must know to take my journey to another level so that one day I can leave and go home? Please, please tell me, O Lord.

When I enter the Kingdom of Heaven to commune with God I know it immediately; the sense that God is present and the sense of oneness is beyond any description I can offer. So it was that morning in Spain as God answered my prayers:

O my child, you must listen for the voice of spirit that will never fail you or lead you to a place that you do not belong. At all times I have taken you in a direction that I know is right for you and in your fear you feel that I have abandoned you. Never, my child, would I walk away from you, leaving you to walk alone and to live in your own shadow, feeling a sense of loss and no future.

At all times I carry you, helping you to gather strength and courage to take with you on your journey. For I have set a course for you, to help you understand your light, your spirit and to find your connection to me. At all times I will be the light guiding you, loving you, encouraging you to be the best and to bring the best out in you.

At all times I will hold your hand so that you will understand that no matter where we go, or how long it takes us to get there, I will always bring you home. For it is there that I have set a place for you, among others to share with them your knowledge, your light, and to show them that they too can take this journey with their own spirit.

So, my child, do not doubt for out there among the stars your journey was set for you and I am with you all of the way, loving you, protecting you and most of all guiding you to a place where you will find your true purpose.

Well, that was that. If I needed to have my doubts dispelled they were now well and truly dispelled. That communication with God also brought home to me once again that there is a divine plan at work, for all of us, and that plan manifests itself here on earth in God's good time.

As the days and weeks went by, one of the most joyous aspects of the move to Spain was the fact that a lot of new angels began to introduce themselves to me. I'd like to take the time now to introduce some of them to you.

I'll start with two angels, Rebecca and Lana. I often refer to them as a double act! These angels have a wonderful soft energy around them and they are full of humour. Indeed, part of their work is to help human beings not to take themselves so seriously. These angels often communicate poetry to me and I've collected numerous poems from them. Sometimes they'll give me a poem that is meant for one particular person, and I've had many grateful people tell me that a particular poem meant so much to them personally, although it may not have meant a lot to me as I was transcribing it.

Another aspect of Rebecca and Lana's work is to help people raise their energy fields. In a way I would describe them as fun angels; their energy blends together in a magical way, it's almost as if they are up dancing in front of you, you cannot help but feel uplifted when they are about.

They don't take things too seriously and they never judge; they're very beautiful angels.

Angel Simone was one of the first new angels to introduce herself to me when I moved to Spain. I'd have to say that Simone mainly works in the background, and by that I mean she can come through when I'm communicating with another angel and I'll become aware of her presence in the background. Or, if I'm communicating with someone who has passed on and I'm having trouble understanding them, I'll become aware of her presence in the background and she'll do her best to clarify things for me. She has a great understanding of human beings' daily lives and our troubles; she's also very practical and is very good at getting down to the nitty-gritty of any problem – in short, she gets the job done.

Simone often appears with Stephen, another angel who manifests as a very big light and a mix of brilliant colours. Both Simone and Stephen will also work with me when I'm in deep sleep. When I wake in the morning I'll have a very vivid image of them both and what they have imparted to me while asleep.

There's no doubt in my mind which angel is the most handsome in the entire angel realm – that has to be Angel Andrew. I've often joked that if Andrew were a man here on earth I'd leave my husband and run away with him! He's a very tall and slim angel, very good-looking and with a wonderful sense of humour. Andrew is full of light and fun and he communicates through the breath. He'll often breathe gently in my ear when I'm asleep to let me know that he's there and my own breath changes and becomes very gentle and slight when I communicate with him. It's difficult to describe just how gentle and understanding Andrew actually is.

If you have any worries in life Andrew will get you to look very closely at them and to understand where exactly the worries are coming from. He doesn't really suggest any remedies but when you really examine what's worrying you the answer appears. Angel Andrew is a very remarkable angel.

Angel Jonathan is another angel who visited me regularly when I first came to Spain. Jonathan has never materialised with wings; he always appears as a man with rather rugged good looks and a very lovely nature. He has an air about him rather like that of a schoolteacher, but a very nice schoolteacher. Jonathan is wonderful in helping me establish a connection with the spirit world, especially if I want to contact a particular person who has passed over. He is a constant source of strength to me, although he can be a little stern at times; he touches the very core of my heart. He's tall, has a husky voice and he often tells me his purpose is to bring me closer to God. I always feel a great sense of peace and purpose when I work with Jonathan.

Then there's Angel Toby, whom I describe as my consistent angel. Toby is a wonderful angel for concentrating your mind, especially if you have a particular task that you need to complete. He gets you to focus very clearly on what needs to be done and he won't let you stray from your task until you've completed it. Toby often speaks to me about the importance of accumulating spiritual knowledge inside yourself. He says that once the knowledge is established in your heart then it will flow out from you back into the world and benefit other people. Angel Toby's light is very special and you can feel it penetrate right through you into your soul.

And I have to mention Angel Anne again; her help in my recovery from illness laid the path for my life's work with the angels. Since moving to Spain her presence has grown and grown. I often joke with her that she likes the warm weather! She'll appear to me first thing in the morning and say, 'Isn't it a glorious day, aren't we so lucky?' But in all seriousness I do believe that Spain and its Mediterranean climate was the right place for me to be at that time. I feel I needed to be in a bright, warm, airy place in order to fully absorb the energy the angels were communicating to me.

It's for a very good reason that I describe Angel Anne as my best friend and if I didn't have her I'd be lost. She's adorable and she gives me a great sense of belief in myself. She's very truthful: she'll tell it to you like it is and she's never in any way negative, but she also has a great capacity to see both sides of every story. Most of all, I suppose she's my energiser. At the beginning of my day I'll say to her, 'I am up and ready to go.' And she'll reply, 'I'm ready too!'

We had been in Spain less than a month and we were really still settling in to our new permanent life here. When you have a holiday home in another country that's exactly how you treat your time spent there – as being on holiday.

We had made friends in Spain with quite a lot of people who had moved from Ireland, and elsewhere in Europe, to live there permanently, but we always had to say goodbye to them when we left to go back to Ireland. Now things were different; we were here permanently and we quickly realised that if this was going to be our new home then we were going to have to treat it like a permanent home.

It was quite strange in the beginning – whereas before we were happy with popping up to the local shops to buy a few things for the house, now we had to establish where the nearest big shopping centre was so that we could shop economically. Little things like that had to be sorted out.

It became obvious to us that we had been living in a very small holiday community before and although we were still there, we now we had to reach out and discover more about the real Spain and that wasn't a bad thing. The Spanish are like the Irish in many ways: they love to stop and chat and they are passionate and friendly people. However, they do love forms! If you have to get anything done in Spain through any government department or local authority, watch out – there will be many, many forms!

It was actually nice getting to know Spain on a new footing. Whereas before we had mostly confined our travels to in and around where we lived, now we were beginning to travel that bit more and see new places. A trip to see the Sierra Nevada mountain range was absolutely beautiful and awe-inspiring. And our first trip to Madrid was really interesting; I immediately liked the city.

Another nice aspect of our permanent move to Spain was the fact that we began to make new friends, some Irish and some from other parts of Europe. We discovered another couple from Norway, Annie and Jan, who were living just around the corner from us although we had never met them before, even though they had been in Spain for quite a while. I didn't know it when I first met them, but Annie and Jan were to play an integral role in what was to become the most important day of my life.

The Spanish love to shop in local markets. Some of them are quite tourist-orientated while others are better value, with some great meat and fresh produce on sale. Annie knew all the good local markets and she suggested that we should make a trip to one about 20 kilometres away. The market was held on a Friday in a village called San Miguel, high up in the hills that surrounded the area where we were living. We started out early that morning and when we arrived at the market there weren't many other people about, which made it easy to browse around all the various stalls and see what was on offer.

I don't know if it's just me, but when I'm surrounded by all that lovely fresh food I tend to go a bit mad and buy more than I actually need. And so it was that morning in San Miguel, as I headed back to the car laden down with goodies, including lovely melons and fresh strawberries that I couldn't resist.

It was still late morning and rather than head straight back home, Annie suggested that we should drive into Torrevieja for some lunch. Torrevieja is a smallish city on the south-east coast of Spain, not far from Alicante and about a 45-minute drive away from San Miguel.

During the summer, when the tourists descend on Torrevieja, it can become absolutely clogged with cars but it wasn't that bad that morning and we had no trouble finding a parking spot just off the main square in the town. We decided we would eat in a small tapas restaurant that we had all tried before. So we settled down at a table out on the street and began to enjoy the whole ambience of the early afternoon. Our food came and it was delicious and quite cheap – unbelievable value if you were to compare it with eating a similar meal in Ireland.

As we had finished our meal, Annie suggested that we should take a walk around the town of Torrevieja. Fran and I had been there several times before but we didn't know the town all that well, so we agreed.

After we had walked for a while we came back to the town square and Annie mentioned that there was a beautiful Roman Catholic church on the square, which was worth a visit because the interior was very beautiful. I've always liked churches, not in any particular religious sense but rather because they are quiet places and I find it's usually easy to let the mind settle down a little in a church, if only for a few minutes. So I readily agreed to go and have a look at the church. Annie was right; the church, the Iglesia de la Inmaculada Concepción, was indeed very beautiful inside. For some reason, as soon as I entered the building I had the desire to be on my own for a little while so I made my way up the central aisle and sat in one of the pews by myself, some distance away from the others. There were only a few other people in the church and as I began to pray a great sense of stillness and peace came over me from nowhere. Then I became aware of a man standing in front of the altar. He was standing about 20 metres away from me and instantly I was mesmerised by his eyes; they seemed to have a hold on me.

Suddenly, everything disappeared. That's the only way I can describe it – the church and everyone in it vanished and I was only aware of this man and his eyes. He was quite young, in his early thirties perhaps. He was thin and he wore a loose-fitting white top. I couldn't really see his lower half. The sense of peace that I felt, just sitting there looking at him, is impossible to describe; I was happy just to sit there for ever more. Then he beckoned to me to come forward, but I seemed to be stuck to the spot. I was frozen – I just couldn't move from my seat.

However, an elderly couple entered the church at that moment and began to walk up the aisle. They genuflected and moved into one of the seats close to the man. Then the man spoke, referring to the couple, 'Look, these people come to me and they do not see. Yet you see and you are afraid to come. Why?' After that, my fear left me and I began to make my way up the aisle towards the man. As I did so, I carried on looking into his eyes and what happened next is difficult to explain. Everything was contained in his eyes: this whole world, the universe and everything in it, was contained in those eyes. Everything was as one and I understood. I understood who I truly am; I understood love, the one love, not human love, not emotional love, but the one love – the love of God. My body was trembling but I had no fear. I was immersed in this state of one love. I asked the man if he was Jesus Christ. I don't know where the question came from; it just came out of me. He replied, 'I am the Son of the Father. I am, that I am.' The words seemed to galvanise me. I don't know how to describe the feeling or sensation that had overcome my body. I seemed to come in and out of it; one moment I was aware of the church and my surroundings, the next I was back in this state of oneness, of total wholeness, of completeness, of total joy.

Then the man took me by the hand, sat me down on one of the seats at the front of the altar and began to explain that I had a journey in front of me, a journey on which I would serve God.

As he spoke, time passed away; everything passed away, everything was as it really is – perfect and whole. It was as if, in an instant, I had this total awareness that we are truly made of God, there is no separation between God and us, there is only ever God. The man continued speaking, and in a flash, quicker than that, I also had this other awareness, an awareness of where human beings go wrong. We go wrong when we think of ourselves as being separate from the Father, separate from God. In that moment I realised it is in fact the only problem that we human beings face – the idea that we are in some way separate from God.

The man then gently placed my hand back down into my lap and said he had to go, but we would meet again. He turned and walked towards the centre of the altar and he disappeared.

I don't know how long I spent on that seat in front of the altar but eventually my friends and my husband approached and asked if I was alright. I didn't know what to say to them, what could I say to them?

We made our way back to the car and started to drive home. Nobody said much on the journey. Although I was the only one who had actually witnessed the man in the church, he seemed in some way to have impinged on everyone's consciousness. It seemed that the silence in the car on the way home was enough for all of us.

I didn't know it at the time but that experience in the

church in Torrevieja was to pave the way for my communication with God on a personal level. The feeling I experienced that day of oneness, of complete love, is the same feeling I experience now when I enter the Kingdom of Heaven when I meditate and talk to God. It can't be described in words, yet words are all we have when we talk to each other about God.

# 14

## Discovering Your Angel

In these days of financial doom and gloom, when the global recession never seems to be far away from all our minds, one very important message I want to get across to people reading this book is the simple fact that each and every one of us can make our own personal connection with our angel.

I'm not saying that if you have financial troubles all you have to do is to open the doorway to the angel realm and all your money worries will disappear. I'm not saying that at all. But each and every one of us has an angel, our own personal angel, just waiting to be invited into our lives to help and guide us in all aspects of our personal life. Our personal angel can help and advise us on our relationships, our employment, our family, our health and prosperity and, most importantly, on our relationship with God. In short, to communicate with your own angel is to believe everything that is already within you.

The biggest obstacle to people opening a personal connection to their angel is the belief that their angel dwells somewhere outside of their own being. Do you believe that your angel dwells up in heaven? Or on the pages of some book or religious text, perhaps even in this book you are reading now? No! Your angel dwells within you, and as a child of God you have every right to call upon your angel any time you wish. If you make this call in earnest and with an open heart, your angel will respond to you.

To seek the daily assistance of your angel is to honour everything already within you so you can begin to better understand the journey that you face in life. At all times your angel will be the closest imaginable link here on earth between you and God. Remember, your angel is already a part of you, that is so important and it is one of the most important messages the angels have for us. When you really grasp this fact you will find you can begin to move mountains and you will also find that it is much easier to love and truly understand yourself.

You will grow and learn about the many beautiful qualities that you already possess within – qualities you've managed to forget about by allowing everyday living, with all its frustrations, thoughts, emotions and worries, to distract you. It is your angel's task to help you clear your mind of all those distractions and return you to the wonderful vibrant living being that you truly are. Your angel carries out this task with relish. She just can't wait to be asked to come into your life and begin to help you – that is the reason why angels exist.

It's quite hard to get across in words just what a difference having your angel to share your life with you actually means. Sometimes, when an angel appears in your life, it can be a very dramatic thing, and all sorts of wondrous, even miraculous things, can take place. But it's also always a very subtle thing, a very gentle thing. Gradually, everything in your life begins to change for the better. You begin to learn and understand why we must have compassion and love in our hearts for everything and everyone around us. You become more confident, more tolerant about things in your life. You become more compassionate, more loving, and you begin to look at things differently. You realise that everything is a part of you, including the angels, that there is no separation; we are all one, one in the same God. This is very, very good news.

You come to understand your life, and what it holds for you, as your angel gently teaches you to have patience and not to always be in a hurry, to take your time, everything will still get done.

You may be someone who has a very busy life. Are you are always in a rush? Perhaps your life is very full at the moment, and you have many responsibilities, a family to look after, a job to worry about – perhaps there are many people who rely on you in one way or another? If any or all of this is true it must be tempting to think that an angel will have a very hard job getting you to slow down and take it easy; life is just too demanding. But that is exactly what will happen if you can just begin to lay the ground-work for your angel to enter your life by becoming still and receptive. Connecting with your angel brings with it a great many experiences, but it is always a subtle and gentle thing. Even the most frenetic of us, constantly running around, always on the go, can begin to learn to let go.

You will begin to learn to listen to that small intuitive voice that lives within you and you will begin to under-stand the true direction of your life. I have often seen the busiest people, who before making that personal connec-tion with their angel were consumed with the everyday chores and worries of living, gradually become more beautiful, compassionate, loving, loyal, understanding and intelligent human beings, and as they learn to love those qualities about themselves more and more their lives become more and more peaceful and secure. It is a subtle and gentle transition.

As you open up your heart to your angel you open your heart to a world full of love, joy, peace, prosperity and abundance. It's not that your angel sends you these things down from heaven or from anywhere else – you already are a child of God and as such all these things already dwell within you: the Kingdom of Heaven lies within you. Your angel's task is to help you realise this simple fact.

To establish that first connection, wait until a time of day when you know that you are going to have some time to yourself, even it is only a few minutes. Now invite your angel to come around you. I want you to feel their presence as they begin to come close to you. Don't be frightened or put off if there appears to be nothing there – there is nothing there – angels arise out of that nothingness.

However, when a connection is made some of you may feel a tingling sensation in your body, see a beautiful light, see a vibrant colour or smell a beautiful fragrance. You may experience a beautiful heat travelling through your body, or a profound feeling of great love may come over you unlike anything that you have ever experienced before. It may be the case that you will become very emotional if you are meeting your angel for the first time. Or you may feel nothing at all, yet you won't regret for a moment having invited your angel into your life.

Just relax, relaxation is very important. When you think

about it, what does it take to really relax – it takes faith, doesn't it? It takes a little faith to let everything go, if only for a few moments. Muster that little bit of faith and you are halfway there to making your personal connection with your own angel. Just allow your angel to come close; remember, angels love to be with us. Now rest for that moment; rest in their love and true essence.

Remember, when you first make contact with your own angel it will be the angel who is closest to you while you are here on earth. Your angel is exclusively interested in your growth and development during your physical lifetime. As you come to know and love them every minute of every day you will be absolutely amazed by the divine communication that allows you to share knowledge and wisdom, which is in fact your own knowledge and wisdom, your inheritance as a child of God.

You may be someone who seems to suffer from negative thinking – no matter how hard you try to rid yourself of it, it always seems to resurface in some way or other. That really doesn't matter to your angel, because all your angel ever sees is the truth of you – you are a child of God, a child of the light and this is your true essence. If you do happen to suffer from negative thinking your angel will help you to find an understanding in your life and a reason for why you are here on earth, and with that knowledge you have the most powerful tool to shift all negative thinking away. Your angel will show you what a wonderful, beautiful and intelligent human being you truly are. If you are feeling very negative it may be that you need to learn how to heal, or how to forgive both yourself and others. Your angel will instantly know what is required and will begin to teach you how to let go, how to find forgiveness, how to have compassion and understanding and how not to judge others or be critical of them. Your angel will gradually help you become a more positive human being.

Angels always have a great understanding of you and what is going on in your life at the present moment. They do not come to live your life for you, they come to assist you and to always help you to find a positive solution to the problems you may be facing at any given time. Angels can teach us about a world of positivity; they can help us to learn to turn our thoughts away from negative thinking and into a more positive way of living and learning. They will show you that your thoughts are powerful and that what we think, feel and say creates our reality – leading us into an area where our lives can be more balanced and centred in everything we do.

Your angel may also give you an affirmation to say. It may be a small prayer or a specific word – whatever is right for you, your angel will guide you to it. The more that we absorb positive thoughts into our consciousness the more we are able to turn our thoughts around quickly from being negative into being something positive. The more we become aware of what we are saying and thinking, the easier it becomes to take our thoughts into an area that is more positive.

Remember, angels aren't constrained by what we call time, the past or the future. So they understand that on this physical plane we inhabit it takes time to change our thoughts into truly positive ones. Therefore angels have great patience with us, especially when we have a tendency to think negatively. If we think negatively we will attract negativity into our lives.

Your angel will help you to truly grow up and for some people that can sound a little scary. But all your angel wants is for you to become a more well-rounded person, someone who doesn't take offence easily and doesn't get jealous or bitter about other people's achievements. When you can see yourself becoming a more tolerant, patient person then you know that you are really beginning to grow up, with the help of your angel.

Although angels are a part of us, because we are all children of God, angels are not like us. They are purely energies of light; they operate on a different vibration level to us but in order to communicate with us they will lower their vibrations so that we can become aware of their presence. So the stiller and calmer we can get our conscious minds the easier it is for an angel to communicate with us.

Nothing is too great or too small for your own personal angel to assist you with. Angels are simply overjoyed to help you, as they guide and direct you. I generally have no special prayers or mantras or anything like that when it comes to connecting to my angels, just whatever comes into my head at any particular time. Sometimes it can be Christian prayers that are very familiar to me, for instance the Hail Mary or the Lord's Prayer. Why do I use Christian prayers to communicate with the angels? Well, I suppose it's simply where I come from. I was raised a Roman Catholic and I do find these prayers very grounding and a great way of connecting and opening up those channels to my angels. But this is my way, if you are of a different faith or tradition use your own prayers, each of us can use whatever suits us best. Whatever you are comfortable with, go with it!

I know from my own experience that when we first open up these channels it is best to keep our prayers very simple; don't get involved with difficult aspects of prayer that you may not have a great understanding of. In short, the more simple the prayer the more effective it is.

As time goes on and you begin to develop more with your angel's help you will find that your prayers will change. You may find that the ones you used in the beginning will no longer sustain you. Remember that there is nothing wrong with any of these prayers but, as you change, they will change too.

When you do open your first connection to your angel and communication begins to occur, it will be a momentous moment in your life. You will be over the moon with joy, the possibilities will seem endless to you and each day will bring new and amazing insights and revelations into your true self. However, you may also encounter some mixed feelings as the mind begins to throw up emotions and fears, and as it tries to create doubts. What will other people, my family and friends, think about me? Will they begin to judge me? Will the angels begin to take total control of my life and will I lose my own personality? What if the angels are all in my imagination – will I be ridiculed? The mind can throw up many questions like this and if these do arise all I can say is to have faith in your angel and persevere. If doubts do begin to surface, and they may not, just rest in your angel's light for a moment or two, ask your angel to come closer so that you can feel a little more secure, and actually feel the sense of wonderment and joy travelling all through your body as the truth of your angel becomes more and more established in your own body. This is a very, very good feeling.

If you have any fears or worries, get them out in the open, put them on the table and hand them over to your angel. It always works, but it works in God's good time, so do try to be patient in all your life's circumstances and in all your dealings with your angels.

Know that your own angel surrounds you and is part of everything that occurs in your life. Your angel can even have an effect on people who may be judging you or giving you a hard time. If the going gets really tough, hold to this great truth: 'All Is One, There Is No Separation.' Repeat it as often as you have to; the power that lies behind those simple words is utterly remarkable.

I'm sure you have noticed, just as I have done, the enormous number of angel books, seminars, courses and even products that are available today. I even saw angel juice on sale in one shop I was browsing around recently – I wonder what that can be! One of the items you will see everywhere in shops and on the Internet is angel cards. I like the idea of angel cards – but why not make your own? I like to make my own cards and I believe they create a more personal touch and your angels actually appreciate them more, as you have put something of yourself into making them. So head out to any of the wonderful art shops around today and get yourself some coloured paper and pens, then sit back and be quiet and await some inspiration to create your own cards – the inspiration will come. When you have created them, why not store them in a special box or wrap them in a favourite scarf? The idea is to make it as personal as you can and your angel will appreciate your efforts.

The angels just love to deal in symbols and signs and as you sit back and trust your angel more and more this will all be reflected in the way you create your angel cards. You will be surprised at what you create through the cards. I became aware that when I started to use the cards certain ones would appear time after time and I began to realise that these cards were beginning to relay a message to me. In order to know the significance of the message I knew I had to communicate more clearly with my angels, in order to understand what it was they were trying to tell me. So yes, angel cards can be very useful in opening that first connection with your angel.

Another very important thing to remember when first communicating with your angel is that angels come to us in our dream state because it is there that we listen, even though we are not aware of it. Our subconscious mind absorbs everything that our angels give to us, allowing the information to be brought back on waking. Keeping a dream journal by your bedside, so you can write down your dream upon waking, may be a good idea. I've found that some dreams can be very precise in the information that is related, so always write down the time and date for future reference.

If you are not sure about something in your life and you need answers or guidance on a particular situation, before you go to sleep at night spend a few minutes talking to your angel. If you need help on a certain matter, say so and ask your angel to be with you during your dreams. Whatever the answer is, it is the right one for you and if you don't understand it, go back to your angel and ask for it to be made clearer to you. Your angel will be only too happy to oblige and assist you.

When thinking about opening up a first direct connection between you and your angel the most important thing to do is to actually begin. This may sound a bit strange but I've come across many people who seem to love the *idea* of angels and all they stand for, yet can't quite believe that they too can have a personal relationship with their own angel. It's as if it's somehow beyond them to make that connection. This is not the truth: your angel stands ready and waiting for you and only you, no matter who you are or what you are, open your heart now and let that divine flow of love begin between the two of you.

Remember that the answers to your questions may come in any of a number of different ways depending on what your angel feels will be beneficial for you at the time. Your angel will always have your best interests at heart and will always guide you to find the right solution to any problems you may have in your life. You may be given a clear direction of where it is you should be going in your life's journey or your angel may solve a problem for you and give you all the correct answers to everything that you have asked. So don't be afraid to take that first step and begin now.

Lastly, I'd like to mention music as being a great help when it comes to opening your first connection to your angel. Music lifts our vibration and it helps us to see and think more clearly. It can take us into a state of awareness where we can feel and sense our angels. Music can also help to take away the daily stresses of our lives; it helps us to let go, to relax and come more into the moment.

When we listen to music, especially soft, relaxing music, it can help to release those blockages in our bodies that prevent and block the voices of our angels coming through to us. It is always a good idea to listen to soft music that you feel comfortable and relaxed with. This can help you to centre yourself. It brings the physical, emotional and spiritual elements of your body into harmony with each other, helping you to open up those channels of communication even more.

Another of my favourite methods of communication is a chant. I use a chant by the Monks of Silas and I have found this type of music to be truly uplifting in my work. Sometimes, when I listen to this music it helps me to see things more clearly and can also give me answers to a specific problem. So before you begin each day, communicate with your angel – just relax and listen to some music and as you continue to do this, you will begin to feel your angel's presence more and more.

# 15

## Meditation and Prayer

You've probably heard and read a lot about meditation and all the various methods by which we can go about learning to still our minds. For my own part, there was only one reason that I began to meditate – I realised that it was necessary in order for me to communicate with the angels more clearly. When I say I started to meditate I feel I should also mention that I started to pray as well. Today, prayer and meditation are two very important aspects of my life.

I've come to know that prayer helps to balance the spiritual mind and the spiritual body. Nobody has told me this and I haven't learned it from any kind of religion or religious books. Anything I've come to know about God, love and life I know because the angels told me. This is how I know that prayer is our link to the source of everything – to God.

It is a link to the divine intelligence that lives within all of us. When we pray we open up our awareness to the light of God that dwells within us. I believe a great many of us pray in earnest and then we can't understand why God does not answer our prayers. Could it be that we are missing the point of prayer? Are we praying to a God somewhere up in the sky or in heaven to do our bidding in some way or other? Perhaps we are missing the fact that the source of everything, God, already dwells inside of us, not up in the sky or anywhere else.

The angels constantly remind me that we are already whole, there is nothing to be added or improved upon, we are all already immaculately whole and present in our bodies and minds, we just need to consciously realise this simple fact. Getting consciously in touch with this divine presence within us is, to me, what prayer and meditation are all about. Each time you begin to pray you heighten your perception of everything and everyone around you. Prayer can help you to find the stillness within that will help you to open up more and more to the great truth of yourself: that God already dwells within you.

In the daily practice of prayer we are opening ourselves up to peace, joy, prosperity and abundance, all the great aspects of ourselves that are already present within us. It is the angels' task to help us realise that the Kingdom of Heaven dwells within us. As we pray and become more and more clear about the truth of ourselves – that God is already present within us – we begin to see more compassion for other people enter our lives, more forgiveness for others, more understanding of others, and more overall tolerance comes into our lives. Not because we have brought it in, but because we realise that it was there all along. We had just, through prayer and meditation, to realise it – to make it real.

When I say that we consciously need to realise that God is already within us, what do I mean by consciously? Many wonderful insights have been imparted to me by the angels during periods of meditation. When I first opened up to the angels, the whole area of consciousness seemed to be a bit beyond me, but one day during a meditation an angel explained to me that consciousness is not only a function of the brain or mind, but is something that exists in every cell of our bodies and in our energetic bodies as well. Consciousness is simply everything, everywhere, and as we truly realise this amazing fact everything becomes more real to us.

A walk in the park suddenly becomes very real, when you look you will realise that everything is alive – the trees, the leaves, the flowers and the grass – you will see them through different eyes; you could say you will see them through your angel eyes. You will become aware that every living thing is a part of you, a part of our consciousness. You will become more caring, more loving and more compassionate.

As the angels make you more conscious, you will realise that there is magic all around you. You will begin to realise that there is a world that lives inside of you and outside of you, yet it is the one world.

Here is an example of how meditation and becoming still within yourself can have amazing results. This wonderful insight came to me completely out of the blue when an angel spoke to me during a short meditation:

Every person, whatever religion or nationality, has an angel guiding them. It does not matter whether you know it or not. We are at all times standing beside you. Whether or not you believe in us does not matter, for we always believe in you. We understand the great many things about you, we sympathise with you, we laugh, we cry with you. We feel what you feel. We watch and we have great understanding of you in your journey of life.

We at all times communicate with you, whether you know it or not. We are there giving you gentle answers to the many questions that you ask. We try to show you the roads to follow so that you won't make the wrong decision. We put you in places that you are supposed to be so that doors can open for you.

We take you away from danger and from making bad judgements. Did you know that? Maybe not! But it does not matter, for we are the guardians of your light.

When you connect with us we rejoice, for you have come to realise the God force that lives in you and you have realised that at all times an angel bestows her love and light on you.

People may laugh at you when you tell them that you seek the guidance of angels, that you communicate on a daily basis with your friends from the light.

Do not judge them or get annoyed with them, for one day they too may open their light to an angel. It's not your job to convince them of the presence of angels. But when they look at you and listen to you there is a chance that they may go away and form their own thoughts on who or what angels actually are and think that perhaps they might have one too!

So you see, when you speak about angels you are actually shining forth a light to others to help them understand about the presence of angels. It is wonderful for us to be able to communicate with you for we have so much to show you.

Every step we take with you is a chance for us to help you understand the wonderful things that are around. We can teach you, we can lead the way, and we can help you no matter what the problem may be.

Sometimes we see you suffering and we pray that you may turn and seek our guidance so that you do not have to suffer alone. Sometimes we cannot fix your problems, for maybe your problem is a lesson in life that you have to learn. But we can guide you to a positive outcome.

We do not come to live your life for you, we ask only to be close to you, to love you, to embrace you in our own light and most of all, to be your friend in times of need, in times of love, to share with you all the joy that we hold for you. We guide you when it is your time to return home to the light, we will show you the way to God, to paradise where you will live forever.

That pearl of wisdom came to me from an angel out of nowhere one day, when I had sat down to meditate for fifteen minutes. I find it just so incredible that an ordinary woman like me can have this kind of living, loving wisdom related to her simply by having enough faith in the angels to be still and just listen.

You mustn't feel that this cannot happen for you, that you are not worthy enough or not special enough. That's just your mind throwing up more of the same old doubts once again. It is truly wondrous what nuggets of wisdom can come through from the angels if we can just have faith and be still and let it happen.

Here is a short meditation that I regularly use and find very useful for connecting directly with my angel presence. I want you to sit in a comfortable chair and be still. Take a deep breath, close your eyes and relax. Now I want you to imagine a brilliant ball of light coming up through the ground, up through Mother Earth. See this ball of light begin to travel up over your feet, your legs, and your thighs. See this ball of light travel up through your spine, your lower back, right into your stomach, up over your heart, your chest, your neck, your throat, your face, your fore- head and right up to the top of your head.

As you visualise this light travelling all the way over you, imagine that your angel is inside this ball of light and as you do I want you to relax for a few moments in this wondrous ball of light. Pause ... now, when you are ready, I want you to ask your angel to hold your hands. When you do this some of you will feel warmth or a tingling sensation. You may see colours form in your mind, feel your hands being gently stroked or just have a gentle sensa- tion in your heart area. For each of us the experience will be different. This is just a simple, but I find very effective, method of helping us to experience the energy of our angel.

Here's another simple meditation that I use and it will work for anyone. Use a pen and paper – it doesn't matter whether you can draw or not, this is just an exercise to bring your angels closer to you, to try and sense them, feel them, touch or hear them. It is enough just to enjoy this exercise as you take part. Just draw your angel the way that you perceive them to be, as a colour, as a person, as a traditional angel with wings or as a light, it's totally up to you. When you have finished, hold the paper in your hand and ask your angel to come around you. Just relax, let everything go, don't be afraid and just see what happens. Some of you may feel your angel stroking you, you may feel their wings around you – that's a real treat! A beautiful scent may come into the room or you may become very emotional and cry. Whatever happens, it's fine just to go with it. Now put your paper down and thank your angel for always being present in your life.

When you first begin to meditate you may find it very difficult indeed because some of us have never tried to sit in silence for more than a few minutes. I was quite like that before I opened up to the angels. You may find attempting meditation very boring or very daunting but, as with beginning many new things, you need to give it some time. If you find that sitting quietly is very hard for you and it begins to feel like a really difficult task, then just get up and walk away and return when you feel a little more rested. Gently does it.

There are an awful lot of books available on different forms of meditation and different techniques. What I've realised is that it's actually very simple – I look on meditation as preparing to have a very close chat with one of your closest friends, your angel. Angels understand perfectly well how the human mind works and how restless it can be. Your angel comes from a place of great stillness inside of you, so if you wish to communicate with your angel it's necessary that you develop some of that stillness consciously. You need to still your conscious mind, at least for a little while. I don't know if it's possible to still your mind completely, all the time, or if that is ever necessary. What I do know is what works for me and, believe me, I'm in no way still all of the time – just ask my husband! But I have been able to achieve a certain stillness within, and so can you. Meditation needs to be given some time, so it's a good idea to dedicate a certain time of the day to doing nothing else but sitting quietly and meditating. How long each day you decide to dedicate is totally up to you but I'd say that if you're completely new to meditation then perhaps ten minutes each day is enough to begin with.

Eventually you will begin to see positive results. One of the greatest benefits that I've received from meditation is that although things that really bug me, still bug me, they don't seem to have the same emotional power as they did before. Stilling the mind seems to take the sting out of a lot of emotions for me. I have achieved this by simply sitting down quietly each day and watching all my thoughts and emotions come and go. I don't try and interfere with them at all, I just sit there and watch. Now my mind, of course, tells me that I should be interfering, I should be doing this or that. In fact, it tells me I should be doing anything except sitting here quietly watching. I'm constantly aware that the angels are there by my side each time I meditate. They just love to sit and watch as I become stiller and stiller – they watch me become more and more a part of them.

Many people put an awful lot of emphasis on visual-ising while you meditate. I have to admit that I found this quite difficult when I first began, but don't be put off. The ability to visualise will come in time, although it may take quite a while. It's far more important, especially at the beginning, just to be able to sit quietly with yourself for whatever period of time you decide. If it all seems too much and you feel you're not getting the hang of it at all, then a good thing to do is to just sit where you are and put your attention on your own breath. After all, meditating is all about entering the present moment and there's nothing more centred on the present moment than your own breath – you're actually breathing in and out life itself. It's a funny thing but you may notice that while you are watching your breath you cannot think at the same time; it's remarkable but it's true, so try it.

Just sit there and watch your own breath for, say, five minutes. It may feel as if you are doing nothing of benefit but that will be your mind that's telling you that. Your mind is wrong; sit quietly in the knowledge that you are breathing in and out life itself, you are centred, you have achieved your goal, you are still.

An area of the body that is very important when it comes to communicating with your angels is the area around your heart. What follows is a beautiful meditation that I use, which has the heart as its centre:

Take your attention to the centre of your heart. Bring a white light down from the crown of your head to the centre of your heart and visualise your heart opening up like a beautiful white rose, opening up further and further. Now lie back into this flower, feel the softness of the rose as you lie into it, feel its petals as they envelop you. The sun is shining, feel the warmth of the beautiful sunlight, let it penetrate you as you fully relax. Now invite your angels to come around you and as they do I want you to hand over any fears or worries that you have at the moment. Hand over everything. If you begin to feel any emotions coming up, just let them happen, do not try to stop them. Remember that your angels have come to help you let go of all your fears, just let everything flow out from you.

When you have done this, rest for a few moments. Now visualise a beautiful ocean in front of you. See the beautiful blue waters coming towards you and allow the waters to come over you. Remember you are safe and well at all times. Just allow the blue water to come up to your neck and know that this blue water will restore and balance your energy, your life. Just rest in the blue water. Now allow the blue water to gently pull back and as it does, become aware of how you feel. Do you feel heavy or light? If you are heavy you are beginning to let go, and that is good. If you feel light you are beginning to trust your angels more and more, allowing them to take away all your fears and worries, and that is also good. Whatever you feel, remember that everything is being restored. Know that at all times you are not alone. You are protected and are being guided at all times.

Now just relax for a moment. Take your awareness back to the centre of your heart and connect with the white light once again and give thanks. Now just quietly relax and get ready to resume your daily life.

If you have just come to meditation you may have experienced some new sensations for the first time. You may have become quite emotional. Don't be concerned about this – it's very normal.

Something else I've discovered about meditation is that

it's always good to get outdoors and meditate if you can. You might think that's all very well for me, living over in Spain with all that sunshine, but I used to do it as much as I could when I was living in Dublin as well. An angel once told me to go outside as much as I could to meditate. She said, 'Take yourself outside and feel the ions in the air, become the air, that's what you are.' I didn't even know what ions were, but I did quickly came to realise that getting outdoors can help you to see things more clearly; it seems to give the mind that bit more space that it needs to let things go.

Often, after I've finished meditating, an angel will give me a beautiful poem. It will usually be Angels Rebecca and Lana or sometimes Angel Jonathan who deliver the poems. The poems are often directed at specific people I know, or to people who may have asked me for a poem from the angels. On other occasions they are simply poems about God, life or the angels' love for all of us. I received this poem after completing the meditation above:

> *O Angel of the light,*
> *Please say a prayer for me.*
> *Please gather all your angels*
> *To come and sit with me.*
> *Tell them to be careful*
> *And to gently ease my way,*
> *For my heart is full of promise*
> *As I sit with you today.*
> *I promise that I'll be the light*
> *That you brought to me today,*
> *And I will try to do my best*

## My Whispering Angels

*To the people that come my way.*
*I promise that I'll open my heart*
*To ease away their pain,*
*And to fill their lives with angels*
*When they call their angel's name.*

# 16

# The Dry Times

It was only when I arrived and really began to settle down in Spain that I fully began to realise the sheer magnitude of the angel realm. I want you to understand that to communicate with angels is to believe everything within you and when you seek the daily assistance of angels you honour everything within you so that you may understand the journey that you face in life.

At all times your angel will be the link between you and God. Angels act as advisers for God so you may come to know, learn and understand your connection at all times to God. Your angel is actually a great part of you. Your angel will communicate with you to show you that as a child of God you are worthy of everything he now gives to you. Each day that you begin to communicate with your angel, you will come to love and understand every part of yourself. You will grow and learn about the many beautiful qualities that you have. You will learn and understand why we must have compassion and love in our hearts for everything and everyone around us. You will come to realise how wonderful and intelligent you really are and if you are not aware of these qualities then your angel will always guide you to bring out the best in you.

Angels will teach you to have patience and not always

be in a hurry. To take your time, everything will still get done. This was a lesson that I badly needed to learn, especially when I first moved to Spain. Angels will help you to listen to that intuitive voice that lives within you, so you may truly understand the direction of your life.

They come to share a belief with you that you are everything God says you are: a beautiful, compassionate, loving, loyal, understanding, intelligent human being and that if you learn to love those qualities about yourself then your life will become more peaceful and secure. When you open your heart to an angel you are beginning a journey that will begin to awaken everything within you. It is a journey that will open you up to new beginnings and new growth, showing you how wonderful your life can be.

However, I would really be disappointed if people reading this book came away with the impression that I am some kind of spiritually enlightened woman who lives in a world surrounded by beautiful angels and doesn't have to worry about the ordinary things in life. Nothing could be further from the truth.

I'm going to tell you about a period in my life that wasn't a particularly happy or positive time for me. In fact, it was one of the worst times I can recall in my whole life and certainly the most difficult time I've had since I made my connection with the angels. It began in October 2006 and lasted three months.

After the angels consciously entered my life I went through a profound period of gratitude; for long periods things were wonderful and each day brought with it new revelations and amazing insights. In fact, some mornings I couldn't wait to be up, out of bed and downstairs to begin meditating, such were the profound feelings of peace, joy and happiness that I would experience once I had opened my connection to the angels.

But then it all changed. I went from the period that I have just described, when every day had a pristine sense of being brand new, to a period of reflection and many months of intensive writing with the angels. I didn't mind the writing, although it involved me going into my room and staying there for three or four hours, taking a break and then returning to work with angels for another similar period. As the angels related what they had to say I would take it all down in long hand. Now I was never the best student in school so the going could get quite tough at times. I also have to admit that sometimes I wouldn't fully understand what the angels were telling me, although they always told me to trust the process and in time I would understand everything they were telling me. 'Trust the process' – that was a phrase that would come to haunt me.

I could sense that a change of direction was coming but I didn't quite know what it was. I had received and transcribed a large volume of work from the angels. The angels had told me that they wanted this work to be delivered to the outside world but they hadn't told me how this was going to be done. An awful sense of restlessness came upon me. I felt a certain disconnection from the angels and I couldn't really see what direction I was suppose to be heading in with them. In short, I became something of a nightmare to be around.

I remember things coming to a head on a plane as I travelled back from Norway to Spain in early October 2006. I had been conducting some workshops in Norway and

Fran had decided to go to England to do a course in massage that he was interested in, so I was left on my own and perhaps it was just as well, given the mood I was in at the time. In the period leading up to this personal crisis I had been very busy communicating with the angels and they had channelled through me this large amount of information concerning what was, in effect, their message for humanity. It really was a lot of information and some days there seemed to be no end to it. But now it all seemed to have come to a standstill and nothing new seemed to be coming in or happening. Looking back on it, I'm a bit embarrassed at how I reacted. I reacted like a little child really. I became moody, grumpy and demanding. I wanted to know what was going on and when things were going to return to normal. Fran returned from his trip to England and he was met with what must have seemed a totally different woman to the one he knew before he left.

'What's the matter?' he enquired, rather bewildered.

'What's the matter? I'll tell you what's the matter,' I blurted out. 'I've given up everything to come on this journey with the angels. I left my home in Dublin, split up my family, came here to Spain where I knew nobody and did everything that I was asked to do and I'm sick of it all now, I'm sick of it.'

Fran just sat there and said nothing. Then he surprised me.

'You just have to trust the process, you just have to trust that the angels know what they are doing. Keep it simple and it will all come right, it has to,' he gently told me.

When I say he surprised me it was because up until now I was the one who was always telling Fran exactly the same thing – that we had to trust the angels, that we had to have faith and to keep going, that no matter how hard it might seem, the angels knew what was best. Now here he was, telling me to do exactly the same thing and boy was it what I needed to hear! I also realised how far Fran had come on his own personal journey with the angels: he too was becoming a completely different person.

The problem was that for what seemed like a very long time – although in reality it may only have been a few months – it appeared to me that the angels were just repeating themselves. They didn't seem to want to engage in anything new and they persisted in relaying information to me that I only half understood. I was becoming more and more exasperated with them and with myself.

Fortunately it wasn't left entirely up to Fran to get me through this apparent desert that I felt I was now stranded in. One evening while I was meditating, an angel appeared to me in my room. I asked her what her name was. 'I'm Angel Abigail and I'm an angel of direction,' came the reply. Well, I thought to myself, direction, I could certainly use some of that at the moment.

'When Fran told you to just trust the process he was right, that is exactly what you must do and continue to do. The message we are relaying to you is divinely ordered, so it must take its own course, not your course, not even our course, but God's course,' explained Angel Abigail. 'You cannot alter it, change it or make it come any faster. You must just set yourself aside and let it manifest; you must bear witness to it. Listen to this message and all will be well. However, know at all times that you are not alone on your journey with us. I'm now going to introduce you to two very special helpers, the Archangels Gabriel and Samuel.'

And with that she disappeared, but I immediately became aware of the two beautiful archangels around me. Their energies were so beautiful and calming that I at once began to feel a little better about things. I actually had always been aware of the presence of Archangel Gabriel and this time, as he came closer, I wanted to know more about him. I wanted a relationship with him so I could understand the purity of his light.

As he came close to me he introduced Archangel Samuel. I had never heard of him before but that did not matter, here he was introducing himself to me and I was more than ready to listen. Both of them then began working side by side with me each day, to help me in that very unsettled and spiritually dry period of my life.

What truly wonderful angels! Their energy was exquisite and both of them helped me to open up to a new vision in my life and to understand my purpose and direction. They helped me to stop looking back over my life, to understand that there were never any mistakes and that the roads we take are where we are supposed to be.

They impressed on me the importance of living more and more in the moment and to appreciate all of the blessings that we have in our lives – the blessings that I had been foolishly ignoring.

Archangel Gabriel's energy was so warm and loving, and so understanding of the fears that we carry in our daily lives. Tears seemed to fall when I communicated with him; it was as if he was somehow opening my eyes through the tears of life so I could see the road ahead more clearly. He had such patience and understanding. He felt like a beautiful warm sunlight penetrating into my very being, bringing feelings of warmth and comfort. There is a wondrous element of God within him and the riches of his light filled me with the oneness that is all of life.

Gabriel is a real charmer: when he speaks there is an air of sophistication around him as if there is somehow a human side to him that also merges with you. His light fills you with the courage and determination to follow your journey through. He has such power within him that it lifts your being, giving you a sense of power so you can walk tall in your life and see your task right through to the finish.

Archangel Samuel is another real character. His laugh is like that of a child who comes to offer you the sheer joy of his light, a light so young and vibrant that it never loses its way or purpose. Samuel's light dances along; he is always on the right road with the most clear intentions of what he is and what he is looking for in life.

Samuel told me to go outside and just listen to the birds sing: it would awaken the softness within my heart – and it did. He told me to just sit and watch a flower, to feel the forces of nature around me. He is such a deep and understanding angel, who looks for the beauty and greatness within everything. His breath is the force of life that emerges within you, helping you to find your way when you feel lost and cannot see the light through the darkness. Sometimes he holds a lantern that is lit by the light of God that lives within us so we may see the road ahead. He rejoices when we listen, he puts stepping-stones in front of us so we may see our way and his laughter is so profound that it touches the very core of our hearts. It felt like having

a great magician within me to have Samuel by my side –
I could achieve anything. His presence is like the rustling
in the branches of a tree, like the wind that howls around
us or like the cat that perches on the window sill; it's beautifully subtle and of the eternal moment. It is like the waves
of the ocean, calling out to us to listen, like the river that
flows by – just a tiny ripple in the beginning but as it flows
it becomes stronger and stronger and it begins to branch
out into something wider and forever flowing. This river
is flowing towards the great ocean of life and each step it
travels before it meets the ocean life will offer it many
lessons.

Samuel told me there will be times when the river will
break away to become a little stream and each stream is a
pathway or a journey that we take to find our true purpose.
There will be many lessons to be learned along the way
and there will be many places we will be guided to, each
one teaching us to have the courage to continue on.

Both Gabriel and Samuel explained to me that one day
I would do the angels' bidding, that I would become a
teacher and go on and help other people to open up and
make their first connection to the angels. Of course, in
order to do all this I had first to understand the angels'
message totally and this was what was beginning to
happen. I was absorbing their message on a very deep
level but my conscious mind was restless and impatient,
and it was making its presence felt in a very negative way.
This was manifesting outwardly as a period of spiritual
dryness.

Angel Abigail had also been present while Gabriel and
Samuel were doing their work, although she had stayed

mostly in the background. Now she spoke: 'There are certain things that you can do to help you become more still, positive and settled as our message unfolds of its own accord,' she gently told me. Then she disappeared again without any further instruction.

But sitting in my room I felt a sense of release, a sense of letting go of my fears and frustrations and a sense of a positive energy returning to me. Thankfully it wasn't long before Abigail returned. I wanted to apologise to her because at one stage I had actually got up and walked away from the angels, such was my frustration with my apparent predicament.

'I'm so sorry,' I blurted out. 'What must you think of me? I must have been a real nightmare to try and work with or even be with.' Abigail laughed.

'You were, but you were a wonderful nightmare,' she gently laughed. It was obvious that she was in a very positive frame of mind now. 'I want you to work on some affirmations,' she told me. 'When affirmations are used correctly they can have a very positive effect on the mind and your self. I'm going to give you a set of affirmations and I want you to get into a certain rhythm of saying them for the next twenty-eight days. You'll be surprised at the outcome.'

This news was so important to me, so precious to me, for I desperately wanted to rid myself completely of the doubts, fears and anxieties that had somehow crept into my consciousness in recent times. So I set about my affirmations with great gusto. This is one of the affirmations that Angel Abigail gave me:

*My thoughts are beautiful and very true,*
*And everything within me is positive too.*
*Divine guidance is a light within,*
*Share those moments when your thoughts run thin.*
*For divine guidance will delightfully say,*
*Let your thoughts be positive as we sit and pray.*
*I do not weep for I am strong,*
*I do not cry when things go wrong.*
*I stand up and firmly say,*
*My life is positive in every way.*

Then Abigail came closer to me and gave me this pearl of wisdom: 'One of the most powerful affirmations that anyone can say is very simply this – "I Am, that I Am, that I Am,"' she whispered. I at once remembered the words as having been spoken to me by the man I met in the church on that unforgettable afternoon in Torrevieja.

'Remember, Francesca,' Abigail gently said, 'I am never Francesca Brown. There is ever only one I and that I is the one source; the one God.'

It's an affirmation that I use constantly, especially if I'm feeling a little negative: 'I Am, that I Am, that I Am ...' Can you feel the energy behind the words? It's truly wondrous.

'Trust the process' – I had grown to dread those three words. However, it wasn't long after I had completed the twenty-eight days of affirmations given to me by Abigail that one morning I woke up with a start in bed and the first thing that came into my mind were those three words. They didn't leave me all day. In fact, they became more and more embedded in my consciousness as the day went on, so much so that several times I sat down and tried to contact Abigail to ask what was happening but she didn't reply. Then, late in the evening, the phone rang. It was Niall Bourke, a journalist friend of mine from Dublin. Niall had some very good news: a publisher in Dublin wanted to publish the story of my life's work with the angels and there was also interest being expressed in publishing all the work the angels had channelled to me. As I put down the phone to Niall those three words – trust the process – were still in the forefront of my consciousness – simple, clear and unchanged.

# 17

# The Ghosts of Normandy

I had always wanted to visit Rome – it seemed such a beautiful city with its exquisite architecture and ancient buildings. I suppose I looked on Rome as one of those special holy places, like Lourdes or Fatima, and I always wondered what it would be like to actually visit the holy city. So my husband Fran and I decided we would do just that.

On 24 June 2007, we set off in our camper van from our home in Orihuela Costa in the south east of Spain, and headed up the coast towards the French border. Had we taken the motorway, the trip would have taken us a mere ten hours, but we chose the scenic route, and the trip would take two days. We were so glad that we did. Our journey first took us through all the beautiful Spanish towns along the east coast, including Alicante, Benidorm, Altea, Denai, Barcelona and Girona. From there we headed into France, through Montpelier, Marseilles, Toulon, Cannes, Nice and Monaco.

You can detect a change in energy each time you cross into a different country, especially if you haven't been in that country before. I had become very used to the passionate, fiery energy of Spain, and when we crossed into France I was instantly aware of a more mellow energy, very lovely. The weather was absolutely glorious – in the mid-twenties and not too hot.

The streets in Monaco aren't wide and we quickly discovered that the camper van wouldn't actually fit down some of them. But, of course, we found this out the hard way, when we got stuck in the middle of one of them! I got out of the van to help Fran reverse back up the street, hoping we wouldn't run into the local police. We giggled like teenagers as we found our way out of that jam: my flip-flop fell off my foot just as I hopped back into the van and Fran took off like lightning – then had to stop as I hobbled back in one flip-flop to retrieve the other. We had never laughed so much.

Our journey continued over the Italian border and into San Remo, Genova, La Spezia and Pisa, and of course, when in Pisa we had to stop and have a look at the leaning tower. It was amazing, and Pisa is a lovely town. We were really beginning to enjoy the freedom of our trip. We continued on through Livorno, visited Elba and then back into Follonica, where we decided we would stay for a few days before heading into Rome. But neither of us could possibly have imagined what lay ahead of us in Follonica.

We pulled into a nice campsite that catered for both tents and vans. It wasn't very full and the manager was a most helpful Italian man with good English. He directed us towards an area where there was only a handful of other vans and tents. As we parked, we noticed another large family group who had already set up camp. There appeared to be about six adults and around eight children in the group, and I instantly liked them. It was just a feeling that these were nice, good people.

We eventually got our van unpacked and began to settle down and enjoy the campsite and the wonderful country-side around us. I felt very happy and relaxed.

In the past, when we had been busy rearing our children back in Dublin, Fran and I had often spoke about getting away and travelling, and Fran had always liked the idea of having his own camper van. When we made the move to Spain, in the wake of my recovery from ME, we had bought one. And, now, here we were in this gorgeous part of Italy in mid-summer with nothing to do except to enjoy the experience.

I couldn't help being drawn to observe the group of people we had first spotted when we entered the camp-site. The children were full of life, running around and playing, while the adults clearly enjoyed each other's company. I couldn't help noticing that two of the men in the group were good-looking, and one especially so, like Robert de Niro but with his hair pulled back into a short ponytail. The women were stylish and all in all they looked like a typical Italian family group.

On the morning of our second day at the campsite I wandered down a pathway that led to some open fields and a small lake. I found a spot by the lake and sat down. I began to reflect on the past four years of my life – it had been such a wondrous journey, and my mind wandered back to that incredible meeting with my little fairy friend in County Wexford and the three wishes he had granted me. Did they come true? Well my first wish that I would establish a stronger connection with the angels had definitely come true. My second wish, for my son Jason to achieve an apprenticeship as an electrician, had also come true. And my third wish that I would one day have my own centre where I could teach the knowledge that the angels had channelled to me? Well, that one was still in the pipeline. But as I sat in the lovely Italian sunshine I gave thanks to my fairy friend and I also made another wish: I wished that if he was ever around my way again he would drop in and visit me; I missed him.

I then decided I would meditate for a little while, and almost immediately a grey-haired, elderly woman entered my consciousness. Her energy shook me a bit and she seemed perplexed and rather agitated.

'Who are you? What do you want?' I asked.

'I am an aunt of Maximus, the one with the ponytail camped next to you,' she replied. I was very surprised.

'What do you want with me?' I enquired.

'Maximus is very troubled and I have a message for him. I beg you to deliver it for me.'

I'm very used to the angel realm and the spirit world asking all kinds of things of me and I'll always do my very best to help if I can, but this task seemed to be beyond my capabilities.

'I don't know your nephew,' I said, 'and I don't speak Italian and I'm on my holidays. I really don't think I can help you.' With that the old lady withdrew from my consciousness but I had a very strong feeling that I hadn't heard the last of her.

That evening, after our evening meal, I began to clear away the dishes and cutlery. As I placed a fork into its tray it jumped straight out and landed on the ground behind me. I nearly jumped out of my skin! I then attempted to put another fork into the same tray and the same thing happened. This time the fork landed very close to Fran, who was sitting on a deckchair.

'What are you doing? That nearly hit me,' he said.

'I don't know. Those two forks have just jumped right out of the tray. I think it's something to do with the old lady who appeared to me earlier today,' I said.

'Oh, don't be ridiculous,' said Fran. And with that he got up and took a handful of knives and forks and began to place them into the tray. But a fork jumped out and went straight over Fran's right shoulder before hitting the ground. This time, we both jumped.

Right, I thought to myself, this is too much; it's time the old lady and I spoke again! I immediately retired into our camper van and went into meditation. She appeared again instantly.

'Well, you've really got my attention now,' I said. 'What is it exactly that I can do for you?'

'Maximus is a senior police officer in Italy,' she replied. 'The reason he is here in this campsite is because he is on sick leave. Another police officer has accused him of doing something that he didn't do. It's been quite a scandal in Italy and has received much attention, but Maximus is a good man and has done no wrong. You must tell him to return to work, and that the officer who has accused him will be found to be lying and fall into disgrace.'

It took a little while to take in all this information, but eventually I said, 'I'll do my best to relay your message, but I still can't speak Italian and that's a big problem.'

'God has many ways, bear with me,' replied the old lady.

That evening was beautifully still and warm and Fran

and I decided we would go down to the lake for a swim. As we approached the lake there were a few people around a little pier that had been constructed so people could dive into the water from it. As I entered the lake a young woman swam by me and called out to her friends who were sitting on the pier. I immediately recognised her accent as being from Northern Ireland. As I began swimming we came close together and I said to her, 'I know your accent. Are you from the north of Ireland?'

'I'm originally from the north,' she replied. 'But I live in Italy now with my husband.'

As she spoke, I realised that I had to ask her if she could help me with the old lady's request.

'Do you speak Italian?' I asked her.

'Yes, I'm nearly fluent in Italian now,' she said.

When we got out of the water I asked her if I could have a private word with her and she agreed. I explained about the Italian family in the campsite and the old lady's request. At first she seemed to be slightly amused by what I was telling her and then she seemed to want to get away from me.

'I don't think I can help you. It all seems very strange to me and none of my business,' she said. Just then, the old lady flashed into my consciousness and gave me a piece of personal information relating to the young woman. She revealed to me about an extension the couple were building onto their home, going into great detail about some of the materials they were using on the project.

This had a remarkable effect on the young woman when I related it to her and she readily agreed to try and deliver the old woman's message to her nephew Maximus. The young woman's name was Maria and I picked up that she wasn't too keen on her husband finding out what we were about to embark upon. But we made our way over to where the Italian family was camped and, as we approached, Maximus came out of one of their vans, looked at us and smiled.

Although I had no Italian I said, 'Maximus?'

'*Si,*' he replied.

I then looked over at Maria and said, 'It's up to you now.' And with that she launched into a two-minute Italian explanation of what I had just finished telling her down by the lakeside. I could understand little bits and pieces of what she was saying just from the sound of some of the words and from her gestures. When she finished, Maximus came over to me and gave me a big bear hug. He was overjoyed and at once went about gathering his entire group around him and relaying what he had just heard. He explained to me, through Maria, that he was a Superintendent in the Italian police serving in Rome and the problems he was encountering with his colleague dated back a number of years. His colleague was corrupt and he had become aware of this, which had caused a lot of upset and tension between the pair, so much so that he had taken sick leave and was seriously considering resigning from his job. But now, on hearing from his aunt – who had apparently passed to the spirit world four years previously – he felt renewed and ready to go back to Rome and fight his case.

He laughed when he heard about the incident with the forks flying out of their tray and said that this was just like his aunt, who was always a very fiery woman when she was alive.

That night, we lit a campfire by the lakeside and opened a couple of bottles of wine. Maximus's friend was another police officer, named Giorgio. We were introduced to everyone in their group and it quickly became clear just what an ordeal Maximus had been going through, having been falsely accused. The poor man was at the end of his tether and it had begun to affect his whole family.

The next day, when it was time to leave Follonica and head for Rome, it was as if we were leaving long-time friends. We hugged and kissed each other and promised to stay in touch.

We moved on to the next leg of our journey to Rome – and if we'd had a lovely time in Follonica and made wonderful friends, unfortunately the same can't be said of our time there. We pulled into a campsite just outside the city and, as it was quite late in the evening, we decided to get an early night and head into Rome the following morning to see the sights.

From the moment I entered the city the next day I had a bad feeling about the place. I suppose the best way to describe it is as an overwhelming feeling of suppression, the energy of the place felt stifled and not free. When we arrived beside the walls of the Vatican City, I couldn't go any further. It was as if a voice was telling me that what lay beyond those walls had not got the best interests of the people at heart. I also had a deep sensation of sadness about the place and a very strange feeling of a great opportunity having being lost. We had been there less than an hour when I turned to Fran and said, 'I really don't like this place and I want to go back to the campsite.' I was born and raised a Roman Catholic – although I don't practise now – and I don't wish to offend anyone, but that was my honest experience of Rome. I have no desire ever to return to the city.

Things picked up once we returned to the campsite and we were eager to get back on the road. We decided to head for Florence. Oh, what a beautiful city! Full of water and locks and very different from any other place I'd ever visited. We sat on Michaelangelo Square, sipped coffee in small cafés and enjoyed some wonderful food. It was blissful.

Next, we headed for Bologna and on to Venice, where we stayed for two days. If you ever get a chance to travel around in your own camper van I'd strongly urge you to give it a try. The sense of freedom that you achieve is remarkable and it really is a different kind of holiday. You get to truly design your own holiday, nothing to do with booking in and out of hotel rooms and worrying about catching flights here and there. We then had an overnight stopover in Innsbruck in Austria, which proved to be a very pretty place. At this stage we decided it was time to think about returning home, so we turned around and began heading back across Europe towards Spain.

However, as we approached France, Fran spoke up with a surprising request. He wanted to extend our trip to see the D-Day beaches at Normandy. We hadn't discussed the possibility of travelling to Normandy when we'd made our original plans, but Fran had served in the Irish Army for over twenty years and had a great interest in World War II and the landings on the beaches. So, as we were already on the road, I readily agreed to extend our trip and head to Normandy.

The French towns of Lyon, Bourges, Nantes, Rennes and Caen sped by. However, the weather had turned against us and it became grey and wet as we approached Cherbourg and Normandy.

If I found the energy around Rome to be very severe and restricting, the feelings I began to experience around Normandy were very different. There was a gentleness about the place and a sense of freedom in the air. The French afternoon was grey and the rain drizzled down.

As we approached a headland that looked out over Utah Beach, one of the main landing places for the Allied troops on D-Day, a very strange thing happened. We could see an elderly man wearing a blue beret about 100 metres away from us. He stood with his face towards the beach. As he turned around and noticed us, we could see that his chest was emblazoned with military medals. He looked right at Fran, straightened up and saluted him. Fran immediately straightened up and saluted the elderly man in return.

It was a very poignant moment and I was lost for words. I just stood there and felt slightly overwhelmed by the moment, as these two old soldiers acknowledged each other as they stood in this remarkable place. The elderly man began to talk towards us and, as he came nearer, we could see his rows of medals and his beret more clearly.

'I think he's a colonel,' said Fran quietly as the man neared us and held out his hand. Fran was right; the man turned out to be a colonel with the French Resistance and that day he was attending a commemoration ceremony with the remaining members of his unit.

As long as I live I will never forget what happened next as we stood on that headland with our new friend the colonel and looked out over Utah Beach. An angel with a brilliantly blue shimmering energy materialised to my left. His energy was very similar to that of the Archangel Michael, although it wasn't him. He looked at us and smiled, then he gestured up towards the sky and my eyes followed. What occurred next took my breath away. A big picture screen appeared, like a movie screen, and I was now looking at the beach in front of me through the screen. As I looked, the clouds parted and a shaft of sunlight streamed down onto the beach. It was like a porthole from heaven, beaming right down. As I gazed at the scene I saw what seemed like hundreds, maybe more, of small energetic entities, pulsating and glowing with subdued colours, mauve, purple, blue and white, all over the beach and the beach-head. Tears began to stream down my face. I couldn't stop them and I didn't want to. I knew these were the souls of soldiers who had died on that beach. I could hear their voices, mostly American or Canadian. They were very young.

The colonel became aware that I was crying and upset and he put his hand on my shoulder to try and comfort me. We then began to move along the beachhead and we came to some of the bunkers that surrounded the beach. I tried to enter one of them but I couldn't do it. The energy changed and I could feel the sense of panic among the young soldiers as they were trapped in those bunkers. It was too much for me and I had to stand back.

As I continued to look out on the beach I became aware of the various manoeuvres that the soldiers had engaged in on that day and how ferocious and deadly the fighting had become. I could hear the voices of officers who were obviously in command urging their troops to move forward, but utter confusion and panic seemed to be everywhere as the soldiers tried to form up and hold their positions. I must have been speaking out loud as the colonel turned to Fran.

'Your wife is a brilliant military historian, it's as if she was here during the landings,' he said.

Fran then attempted to explain to the colonel about my relationship with the angels and their ability to show me events from the past and the future. I'm not sure how much he actually took in but he took both of my hands in a strong grip and, with tears in his eyes, he kissed me on both cheeks.

With that, the angel with the brilliant blue energy materialised again. Looking at the three of us, his energy sparkled and he smiled warmly. Then he spoke: 'The road to freedom is the road to your heart.' That's all he said and, with those words, his beautiful energy began to slowly fade away into the greyness of that French afternoon.

I'm not a political person, nor even particularly interested in history, but what happened on that afternoon in Normandy was one of the most emotional and strangely uplifting experiences of my life. I will never, ever forget it. It took us another two days to get home to Spain but the experience of Normandy was still very much with me when I walked into our house in Orihuela Costa. If it's God's will, I'd like to return to Normandy one day.

Angels are always trying in their own way to help us learn from our past. My lasting impression of what happened in Normandy was, unsurprisingly, just how tragic it was that all those young lives had to be lost. But there was also a very definite impression that it was not for nothing, and that a very important turning point in our history was achieved.

The angel who appeared to me that day made the point about the road to freedom being the road to our hearts. There are two types of freedom. We all desire to be physically free and man has fought for that right down the ages. Wasn't that what Normandy was all about? But there is also spiritual freedom. We all desire this as well, although some of us are more aware of this fact than others. Spiritual freedom cannot be explained in words; it's beyond words. But the amazing thing that I really want to convey to anyone reading this book is that these wonderful creatures of light, angels, are available to each and every one of us to help us achieve spiritual freedom while we are here on earth.

I can guarantee that anyone who takes the time to sit quietly in their room, even for ten minutes each day, allows their mind to become restful and puts their trust totally in the angels, will very soon receive a sign. An angel may not materialise in their room in front of them – or perhaps it will – but they will definitely receive a sign. A gentle voice somewhere in the back of their mind may utter a word of advice. Or a physical sign may occur. I remember that when I first began to open up to the angels I would sometimes be thinking of something quite important, at other times of something insignificant, but that very thing would pop up in front of me on the television or radio. At other times, while reading the paper my attention would be drawn to a certain newspaper article that contained a message for me. The more I trusted in the angels the more it happened.

Any idea that a person has to be psychic, clairvoyant or

somehow 'blessed' to communicate with angels is total nonsense. And anyone who tries to tell you that you have in some way to be a special person before you can communicate with angels has a lot to learn about the truth of angels. Isn't it remarkable that these wonderful creatures of light, which emanate from the source of everything – God, are at hand to help us if people can just muster enough faith?

# Epilogue

# Angel Verse

A very important aspect of my journey with the angels is the fact that they are constantly relaying poetry to me. Now, don't get me wrong, when I say poetry I'm not suggesting that I am in some way a brilliant poet. I'm not suggesting that I'm even a good poet. What I am saying is that I've witnessed many times the comfort and even feelings of joy many people experience when they receive a poem from the angels – it's remarkable. Perhaps a better term for a lot of what the angels give me is 'angel verse'.

Although many angels have given me beautiful poems over recent years, three angels in particular seem to specialise in poetry. These angels are Rebecca and Lana, who always appear together, and Angel Jonathan. At first, when Rebecca and Lana told me that they would be coming through to me with poetry I thought to myself, 'Oh these are all going to be light-hearted humorous poems,' simply because both Rebecca and Lana are such funny and humorous angels. But it hasn't proved to be the case that all their poems are humorous. They've actually given me what, in my opinion, are some of the most beautiful, simple and heartfelt poems. A lot of people comment on how childlike the poetry is and I agree with them: it is childlike, simple and very innocent.

I once asked the angels what the purpose of all the poetry was. This was at a time when they were giving me a great many poems, so many in fact that it was quite a task to take them all in and get them down on paper.

'To heal and comfort people,' was the reply I was given. Ever since that day I've never questioned the amount of poetry that is given to me but I have witnessed the great healing and comfort that many of the poems have brought to a lot of people in many different ways.

For some time I just used to write the poems down, record the date and time they came in and store them away. If some of the poems meant something to me personally I might have them framed and hang them on my wall at home or if they were intended for a specific person I'd make sure that the person got the poem. But one day, Angels Rebecca and Lana took me to task about the whole question of poems from the angel realm.

'The poems were not meant to be kept away from people. You don't hide them, you pass them on,' I was told in an unusually stern voice. They explained to me that every poem was actually meant for some individual. Some were meant for individuals I'd never met and wouldn't meet, but they also explained to me that one day all the poems they had given me would be published and brought to a much wider audience. How or when, I've no idea – they didn't say.

Poems can come through to me at any time of the day or night and in any given situation or place. Very often I'll just get the first line of a poem in my consciousness and I'll head for somewhere quiet where I can get the rest of it down on paper. I've had poems come through to me when I'm out cutting the grass or doing my weekly wash. I'm sure people have thought me completely insane as, out of the blue, I exclaimed, 'Where's my pen and paper?' and headed off to my room! For various reasons some poems stay in my memory after I receive them. I recall the angels once giving me a beautiful poem relating to a young cousin of my husband. This young man happened to be starting off in a career in acting and the poem came from his grandfather through the angels. It is entitled 'For A New Rising Star':

*When my grandson was born*
*He had a twinkle in his eye*
*He was given the magic*
*And told that he could fly*
*Fly with the birds*
*And with his angels true*
*For he's a star in heaven*
*And a bright star too.*
*You have been given a gift*
*To bring magic to the screen*
*To light up the many people*
*Who love to await the next scene.*
*You have a talent deep inside*
*That will take you very far*
*Over all the green hills*
*And up unto the heavens where you're a star.*
*But in all of your journeys*
*From now until then*
*Believe in your Grand Dad*
*Your Grand Dad Jem.*

Here's another poem I received from the angels. I think it's wonderfully reflective and points to the simple truth that God already dwells within us. It is called 'Room with a View'.

> *I often wondered what I'd do*
> *If I had a room with a beautiful view*
> *Would I sit up late*
> *And watch the stars*
> *Twinkling lightly towards my heart?*
>
> *Or would I capture the moment*
> *Of the beauty outside*
> *Breathe every breath*
> *With the mountains at my side?*
>
> *Would I look way out*
> *Far and beyond*
> *And listen to the stillness*
> *That lies out beyond?*
>
> *But do I really need a room with a view?*
> *For one already lies*
> *Inside of you.*
> *It lies inside your beautiful heart*
> *It's a window to the light,*
> *From the dark.*

I'd like to mention one very special poem that I received from the spirit world. Again it concerns a relative of my husband Fran. It came from a fourteen-year-old girl called

Sinead and was dedicated to her mother Maggie, a cousin of Fran's.

I awoke one morning to find a lady standing beside my bed. She was with a gentleman and a young girl. I asked the lady who she was and she replied that her name was Peggy and she was an aunt of Fran's. She introduced the other two people as her husband and her granddaughter Sinead, who were with her in the world of spirit.

I became aware that the granddaughter was holding the hand of her grandmother, which made me feel that they had been very close when they were here on the physical plane.

Peggy continued to talk and explained to me that she had a daughter still living called Maggie and that she wanted Maggie to know that her mum, father and daughter were doing absolutely fine in the spirit world.

I also noticed that the lady had in her hand a gold bracelet, which she kept dangling in front of me and smiling. I would not understand the meaning of the bracelet until the message was relayed to her daughter.

Although Fran had not seen his cousin Maggie for some time he went in search of her and eventually found her. When he related the message that the family were all together in the world of spirit and doing fine she was over-joyed. Fran also asked her about the bracelet her mother was holding and Maggie explained that on the death of Sinead her father bought two gold bracelets, one of which he gave to her and the other to her mother, Peggy, who was still alive at the time.

A short time later, Peggy and Sinead visited me while I was sitting in my back garden. This time it was Sinead who spoke and she gave me a beautiful poem to give to her mother Maggie called 'Mama I Miss You So'.

*Mam, if I could go back*
*To that very day*
*I would have asked the angels*
*To let me stay.*
*I would have held out my hands*
*And said please don't let me go*
*For this is my mammy and I can't let go*
*But the angels knew what was best for me*
*And they told me to be strong*
*And to be strong for thee.*
*This child we take is one of the best*
*She's been chosen by God*
*To be an angel of rest.*
*She'll come to you*
*When you're not quite sure*
*She'll whisper in your ear*
*Mam, I am just here.*
*Mam, if you listen you can hear my voice*
*A sweet melody, which is always your choice.*
*I sing to you every day*
*I even sing when you pray.*
*So please, Mam, don't cry no more*
*For I am here in heaven, just at your door.*
*When I ring the door*
*You will see*
*Mam, you were special*
*You and me.*

I believe that this simple poem is a wonderful illustration of how the bond of love never dies between human beings once we are open to the spiritual impulse. Here's another wonderful poem that deals with the majesty of nature and of God. It is called 'Spirits in the Wind':

*I am walking outside in the beautiful air*
*Listening to the birds as they sing in the air.*
*I am looking around to all of the trees*
*As they gently blow in the warm summer breeze.*

*I am listening to my footsteps as I am walking along*
*They have a beat and it sounds like a song.*
*The words they are saying are just for me*
*As I gently walk with all of thee.*

*Breathe in the air that keeps you alive*
*And you will feel spirit move inside.*
*Listen to spirit as he walks with you*
*For he is one with nature and you are too.*
*Listen to his words as he whistles in the wind*
*All about you and the journey within.*
*Treasure your walk each and every day*
*For you are one with nature*
*As you go on your way.*

I know that for a great many people the whole area of healing, whether it is for themselves or their loved ones, is very important. Here is a beautiful little poem that came through to me one day and is a wonderful way of asking for healing. It is called 'Prayer Before Healing':

*Dear Angel of healing*
*Please sit beside me*
*Help me to be strong*
*So I can work with thee.*
*Guide your energy through my hands*
*So I will have the strength*
*To heal with my hands.*
*Stay with me every day,*
*Listen to me, when I pray*
*Take all my fears, away from me*
*So I can truly work, with all of thee.*

This is a lovely poem given to me by Angel Rebecca. It is called 'The Love of an Angel':

*The love of an angel*
*Is a wonderful thing*
*She comes from a light*
*That never lets go*
*To help you believe*
*In the things you know.*
*She gives you the courage*
*To stand very tall*
*And to make the right choices*
*So that you won't fall.*
*And for all of the things*
*She guides you to do*
*The love of an angel*
*Is the wonder of you.*

This little poem came to me while I was just sitting quietly by a small river one day. It is called 'Dear Lord':

## Angel Verse

*I am sitting outside*
*Beside a beautiful tree*
*And the river is flowing*
*Just beside me*
*The birds are singing*
*In all of the trees*
*And the wind is blowing*
*All around me*
*I am sitting here quietly*
*In all of my thoughts*
*Thinking what would I do*
*If you sat beside me?*
*Would I run and hide*
*And feel very shy*
*Or would I welcome you*
*With a wink of my eye*
*It doesn't really matter*
*What I do*
*For the river is telling me*
*That it is already you*
*You're flowing by*
*Like a river of light*
*Smiling at me*
*Through the sky at night*
*Your listening to all of my*
*Thoughts in my head*
*And giving me the answers*
*that is inside my head*
*So dear Lord*
*Please sit beside me*
*Under the beautiful big old tree*

Lastly, this is one of my favourite poems. It is called 'Touched by an Angel':

*I was touched by an angel*
*Today you know*
*She knocked at my door to say hello*
*She stepped right in*
*And sat right down*
*And a beautiful light, went all around*

*She said she had come from the beautiful blue sky*
*To live with us until the day we die*
*She will walk with us, along the way*
*And she will help us grow as we go on our way*

*She is a beautiful angel*
*With a beautiful light*
*And she glows like the stars*
*In the dark of the night*

*She is a beautiful friend*
*Who will travel with you*
*As you walk the path of life*
*That was set for you*

*When you are touched by an angel*
*Remember one thing*
*It's like a light*
*Switching on, from the outside to the in.*